I warmly commend this e_____
1 Peter. Angus Macleay p_____
and shapes of the letter, _____
details of the text and also offers much help___
how to apply and present its material.

Vaughan Roberts,
Rector of St Ebbe's Church, Oxford
well known author and conference speaker

This volume is full of practical help for teachers and preachers, and the careful exposition of the text draws out powerfully its relevance for the 21st Century Western Church.
This must be added to your library.

Peter Maiden,
International Director of Operation Mobilization
Chairman of Keswick Ministries

As Rector of St Nicholas Sevenoaks, Angus has plenty of
experience in preaching to a large and biblically literate congregation. He is, therefore, an entirely appropriate person
to write a commentary on a book of the Bible the express
purpose of which is to show preachers how to preach. All
good preachers are also good learners and will welcome
such an approach.

Quite fittingly, Angus has confidence in the Word of
God, as found in Scripture, at the centre of his concern.
He is meticulous in his attention to the text; its setting,
background and meaning. But he also wants to proclaim
its message to our world today. He wants to bring out the
Word's meaning, challenge and comfort for us.

He notes that 1 Peter is addressed to those Christians
who were on the verge of a great persecution, but who
were already experiencing exclusion, hardship and hatred
for the sake of the Name. Even while at home in their own
cities, towns and families, these Christians were feeling that

they were exiles in a strange land. Their situation has an uncanny resemblance to our own where, in a culture that is rapidly moving away from its Christian foundations, we have to learn to be both citizens and exiles, to belong and not to belong, to seek the welfare of the city but also to be prepared to stand up for the faith and its implications in daily living.

Peter is writing as the fellow-elder and witness to Christ to other elders and their churches. Angus brings out the uniqueness of this letter, while also relating it to other parts of the Bible. He wants us to appreciate 1 Peter's special approach, whilst seeking to relate this to the mind of scripture as a whole.

The commentary is vigorously theological but it has many practical suggestions about how to organise a sermon series or a season's Bible study and whether to be thematic in approach or to concentrate on a systematic exegesis of the text.

In whatever way we use this commentary, we will find it profitable for teaching, instruction, correction and encouragement.

Michael Nazir-Ali
Bishop of Rochester

TEACHING
I PETER

Unlocking 1 Peter for the Bible Teacher

ANGUS MacLEAY

SERIES EDITORS: DAVID JACKMAN & ROBIN SYDSERFF

PTMEDIA

CHRISTIAN
FOCUS

Unless otherwise indicated all Scripture quotations are taken from the Holy Bible, New International Version. Copyright © 1973, 1978, 1984 by International Bible Society. Used by permission of Hodder & Stoughton Publishers, A member of the Hodder Headline Group. All rights reserved. 'NIV' is a registered trademark of International Bible Society. UK trademark number 1448790.

Scripture quotations marked ESV are taken from *The Holy Bible, English Standard Version*. Copyright © 2001 by Crossway Bibles, a publishing ministry of Good News Publishers. Used by permission. All rights reserved.

Scripture quotations marked KJV are taken from the *King James Version*.

Copyright © Proclamation Trust Media 2008

ISBN 978-1-84550-347-5

10 9 8 7 6 5 4 3 2 1

Published in 2008
by
Christian Focus Publications Ltd.,
Geanies House, Fearn, Ross-shire,
IV20 1TW, Scotland, Great Britain
with
Proclamation Trust Media,
Willcox House, 140-148 Borough High Street,
London, SE1 1LB, England, Great Britain.
www.proctrust.org.uk

www.christianfocus.com

Cover design by Moose77.com
Printed by Nørhaven Paperback A/S, Denmark

All rights reserved. No part of this publication may be reproduced, stored in a retrieval system, or transmitted, in any form, by any means, electronic, mechanical, photocopying, recording or otherwise without the prior permission of the publisher or a license permitting restricted copying. In the U.K. such licences are issued by the Copyright Licensing Agency, Saffron House, 6-10 Kirby Street, London, EC1 8TS www.cla.co.uk.

Contents

SERIES PREFACE

Whether you are a preacher, a small group Bible study leader or a youth worker, the *Teach the Bible* series will be an ideal companion. Few commentaries are written specifically with the preacher or Bible teacher in mind, and with the sermon or Bible study as the point of reference. The preacher or teacher, the sermon or talk, and the listener are the key 'drivers' in this series.

The books are purposefully practical, seeking to offer real help for those involved in teaching the Bible to others. Section One contains basic 'navigation' material to get you into the text of 1 Peter. The two introductory chapters are: Getting our Bearings in 1 Peter (key themes, structure, literary style etc.), and Planning a Series on 1 Peter.

One of the suggested series provides the framework for the meat of the book in Section Two, with a separate chapter devoted to each sermon, talk or Bible study. The content of these detailed chapters is neither commentary nor sermon, but specifically geared to help the teacher get to grips with the text with its intended purpose clearly in view, its proclamation as the living Word of God. Chapters follow a consistent structure: 'Listening to the Text', 'From Text to Teaching' and 'Proclaiming the Message' (which includes a suggested preaching outline and format for a Bible study).

We are delighted that Angus MacLeay has written Teaching 1 Peter for the series. Angus wrote the first draft of this book while on sabbatical, and then preached the material at St. Nicholas Sevenoaks and at a number of conferences. The result is a well-worked manuscript, written by a preacher, for preachers!

Our thanks to Katy Jones Parry, Zoë Moore, Moira Anderson, Anne Sydserff and Sam Parkinson for editorial assistance and, as ever, to the team at Christian Focus for their committed partnership in this project.

David Jackman and Robin Sydserff
Series Editors, London, December 2007

AUTHOR'S PREFACE

Towards the end of my first academic year at theological college in 1986 I attended a conference organised by The Proclamation Trust. That conference was formative in a number of ways. Through the talks I was able to gain a much more coherent understanding of the whole Bible and how the various parts functioned together. Through the workshops I was exposed to a rigour in handling the biblical texts which I had not known before. Through the friendships established over those few days I have since received enormous encouragement in my gospel ministry.

Since that conference I have often been grateful for the ministry of The Proclamation Trust and for the way it has sought to model the careful handling of God's Word so that God's voice can be heard. I have constantly been challenged to listen afresh to the Scriptures and to be more sensitive to the genre or setting of a particular text.

It is now my privilege to contribute to this series commissioned by The Proclamation Trust. My desire is to pass on to others some of the lessons I have learnt through its ministry over the years. In particular, I hope that preachers will be able to pick up the thought flow of the letter (what is often called 'the melodic line') and recognise the importance of the context into which Peter was speaking as a way of unlocking the letter's significance for our own generation. The introductory chapters should help preachers get their bearings in 1 Peter and help them see how they could plan a preaching series on this epistle.

I believe that 1 Peter has a special significance for our times. Peter was writing into a situation where God's people were beginning to experience opposition and persecution. His letter not only highlights the privileges available to the believer both now and in the future, but provides practical help and encouragement, undergirded by a rich Christology, concerning how the believer should live and work in a world which was sometimes appreciative of the presence of Christians but was becoming increasingly hostile. Such is our world today in the West and it is vital therefore that we heed the lessons of this wonderful epistle.

This book was almost not written at all. Originally I had plans to spend a short sabbatical in 2006 observing a number of churches in North America. However, a severe illness the previous year derailed those plans, so that as the study leave started I found myself working on 1 Peter in preparation for a sermon series at St. Nicholas, Sevenoaks. Part way through my sabbatical an encouraging meeting with David Jackman gave me the impetus to turn my research into a book and since then I have been grateful for the constant encouragement of the staff at The Proclamation Trust – in particular David Jackman, Robin Sydserff, Zoë Moore and Katy Jones Parry for their thoughtful interaction and editorial assistance. I am also indebted to the Church Family at St. Nicholas Sevenoaks who have supported me in this project through their eagerness to hear and engage with God's Word preached, with particular thanks to my personal assistant Margaret Marshall for typing successive drafts of the manuscript. I am grateful to my children, Rachel and Jamie, and especially to my wife, Sue, who have given me every encouragement in my ministry and it is to them that this book is dedicated with my love.

I trust that you will find this book a help as you seek to be a faithful and engaging preacher of 1 Peter.

Angus MacLeay
St. Nicholas Sevenoaks
Christmas 2007

DEDICATION

for Sue, Rachel and Jamie

SECTION ONE:

Introductory
Material

I

Getting our Bearings in 1 Peter

1 Peter is one of the treasures of the New Testament. Tucked away at the end of the New Testament after Paul's epistles, it makes an important contribution despite its brevity and deals with a number of extremely significant issues. It firmly focuses the believer on heaven and the appearing of our Lord Jesus Christ, helping us to cope with the suffering which comes to believers by showing us how such a path can lead to glory. And all the time, despite this future perspective, it is full of practical assistance and guidance as Peter wrestles with the everyday realities of how the believer should live in an ungodly world. Peter's theological vision is centred on the person of the Lord Jesus Christ whom he knows as the risen, living Lord and Saviour who will one day appear as the Chief Shepherd to gather His flock. His great concern is that in every situation believers may be found following Christ, imitating His life and behaviour

so that one day they too will move from suffering, to glory. If, therefore, you want to preach on a book which will focus on Christ and assist believers in living as Christians amidst opposition and suffering then 1 Peter is an extremely appropriate choice.

The apostle Peter

The book starts by introducing the author as the apostle Peter, known to us already through the Gospels (1:1). Elsewhere he refers to himself as an elder who has shared in the sufferings of Christ (5:1 – see ch. 17). Despite his weakness, evidenced in his betrayal of Christ, the Acts of the Apostles reveals how he has been changed into a Christian leader willing to stand and embrace suffering for the sake of Christ (e.g. Acts 4:19, 20). Acts also reveals his role in enabling Gentiles to become fully fledged members of the church, which is an important point to note when we come to consider the recipients of this letter.

Peter is partnered by Silas in the practical writing of the letter (5:12) and is almost certainly based at this point in Rome – though he chooses, for theological reasons, to entitle the city 'Babylon'(5:13) as an indication that like Christians all over the world he was still, for now, in exile.

Sources suggest that Peter died in Rome, probably at the hands of the Emperor Nero some time after the fire in Rome in AD 64. Since Nero died AD 68 it is likely that the letter was written at some point in the mid-sixties. Whatever the exact date, it is almost certain that Nero was emperor at the time of writing, which gives added extra significance to the encouragements at 2:13-17 for Christians to honour the emperor.

Peter's recipients

The .people to whom Peter wrote lived in a number of territories mentioned at 1:1 – Pontus, Galatia, Cappadocia, Asia and Bithynia. Together, these five territories form a large part of the modern state of Turkey and all were within the bounds of the Roman Empire. The gospel may have come to these areas through converted Jews returning from Pentecost after hearing Peter's sermon (see Acts 2:9), but we know from Acts and Galatians that much of this area was later evangelised by the apostle Paul.

Though there may well have been a mixture of converted Jews and Gentiles within these churches, 1:14, 18 and 4:3-4 suggest that it is likely that the majority were from a Gentile background. Though not conclusive, it is unlikely that Peter would refer to converted Jews as having been 'redeemed from the empty way of life handed down to you from your forefathers'. Also, the activities described in 4:3 – which equate to 'the flood of dissipation' of 4:4 – would have been abnormal for the Jews.

Peter is probably, therefore, writing to converted Gentiles with no spiritual pedigree, on the very edge of the empire, wanting to show these insignificant, small and persecuted groups that in God's eyes they are His chosen people – the centre of His eternal purposes.

Peter's epistle

The letter is relatively short at just 105 verses in our Bibles. It bears the traditional marks of an ancient letter with its introduction and greetings at the start and words of farewell, encouragement and blessing at the end.

A letter would have been written at a particular time and for a particular purpose, even if the recipients were scattered in various communities many miles apart. It is likely, as the exposition will highlight, that the growing pressures, ranging from ostracism and verbal abuse to physical persecution, were the occasion for Peter's word of encouragement to them.

In any letter it is not surprising to find order, purpose and development, and that is certainly the case here, since Peter has the clear aim of helping embattled Christians to keep following Christ all the way to glory.

Peter's message

The brief introduction at 1:1, 2 provides hints concerning the overall structure of the epistle. Peter describes these Christians as God's elect – His chosen people – and this is the main theme which undergirds the first section of the letter (1:3–2:10) culminating in the statement at 2:9, 10 'you are a chosen people'. Within the Old Testament we see God's chosen people emerge from Egypt following the Passover sacrifice. They are constituted as God's covenant people and then start their trek through the wilderness to the Promised Land. Peter envisages the same model for Gentile Christians as for God's chosen people in the Old Testament (see ch. 3) and many of the Old Testament quotations and allusions within this first main section are to the Exodus.

Returning to 1:1 we see that God's elect are also exiles or strangers. This theme is developed in Peter's second main section (2:11–4:11). There is a natural link between sections 1 and 2 since, if their true home is in glory, it means that their current living quarters must not be regarded as 'home'. This is a natural development from the theological weight put upon the future in section 1. Section 2 of Peter's letter is therefore devoted to working out in practical ways how the Christian lives as an exile within a society where God is not obeyed. Time and again Peter applies the pattern outlined in 2:11, 12 (turn from sin, seek to do good … and trust God for the results) as a model for Christian behaviour in the world. Towards the end of this section Peter also deals with the issue of how Christians should respond to opposition they faced even when they seek to do good; this is answered at 3:13–4:6.

It seems natural to identify 4:12–5:11 as a third main section of the letter (see ch. 16). However, amongst the commentators there is no clear consensus about how this final section fits together and brings it to a conclusion. My own view, developed within this book, is that the common thread linking the various units within Section 3 is the theme of Christ's sufferings. 'Sufferings' occurs in the plural three times (4:13, 5:1 and 5:9) and refers to the suffering which believers may face specifically as followers of the Lord Jesus Christ. Though God's elect (Section 1) are seeking to live for God as exiles in a hostile world (Section 2) they are to be reminded that there is a basic pattern for their Christian experience (Section 3), though you follow Christ now in His sufferings, you must keep following Christ because it will certainly lead to sharing in Christ's glory at the end (see 4:13; 5:1, 4 and 5:10). Section 3 therefore provides a fitting climax and conclusion to the whole letter, highlighting Peter's theological insistence that the whole of the Christian's life is to be shaped by following Christ through suffering to glory.

So, we have identified three main sections and three main movements within 1 Peter. Each is connected and develops from the other to provide a coherent framework for the Christian life which addresses the particular issue of opposition and persecution. It is vitally important therefore as a preacher to keep this big picture in mind, so that each passage can be seen in the light of the overall message.

Peter's conclusion (5:12-14) brings together various greetings; it is also linked to the opening (1:1, 2) with its references to God's 'chosen' people residing in 'Babylon' (elect exiles), and sums up what Peter thought he was doing. What he has written is an encouragement for them to keep standing in the true grace of God. As we preach 1 Peter our aim must also be to encourage God's chosen people, currently in exile, to keep standing firm as they are buffeted by all sorts of pressures and opposition to the Christian faith, because as they follow Christ even amidst their sufferings they will soon share in His glory, through God's abundant mercy and grace.

Outline of 1 Peter

The following provides a brief outline of the main divisions of 1 Peter which are explored within this book. As has been argued, Peter operates with a clear structure in mind. His three main sections are all quite different in their approach, though there are important links between them.

Introduction: God's people: chosen and in exile (1:1, 2)
Section 1: God's people: chosen for glory (1:3–2:10)

    1:3-12   Remember where you're going
                (future privileges)
    1:13-21 How do you get there?
    1:22–2:3 How do you keep going?
    2:4-10   Remember who you are
                (present privileges)

Section 2: Living as exiles in a hostile world (2:11–4:11)

    2:11, 12 Introduction to Peter's strategy
                for Christian living
    2:13-17 … in the world
    2:18-25 … in the workplace
    3:1-7   … in the home
    3:8-12   … in the church
    3:13-22 How to cope with direct persecution
    4:1-6   How to cope with indirect persecution
    4:7-11   How to cope together as God's people

Section 3: The pattern for Christian living; from suffering to
*   glory through following Jesus Christ (4:12–5:11)*

    4:12-19 … as those who suffer
    5: 1-4 … as those who lead the flock
    5: 5-11 … as those within the flock

Conclusion: 5:12-14

2

PLANNING A SERIES ON 1 PETER

One of the practical issues facing the preacher committed
to the expository method concerns the division of a book
of the Bible into appropriate sections. A number of factors
must be considered:

+ Would the congregation benefit more from an overview of the letter taking only a few sermons or by
  allocating plenty of time to the detail of the letter?

+ How long would the congregation be able to cope
  with a particular series?

+ Are there any practical constraints which need to be
  borne in mind, e.g. a time frame such as an academic
  term, church diary constraints due to special events
  or holidays, preaching allocations (if there is more
  than one preacher available)?

A number of possible series are listed below, ending with the
longest which is the basis for the expositions which follow.
In each series the intention is to work with the structure
and flow of the epistle.

Series 1. Three Sermons

Sermon 1	1:1–2:10
Sermon 2	2:11–4:11
Sermon 3	4:12–5:14

Clearly the aim here is to provide a brief overview of the whole letter. This is a short series using Peter's three sections as its main structure. Sermon 1 could use material from 1:1, 2 and 1:3-12. Sermon 2 could use Peter's strategy outlined at 2:11, 12. Sermon 3 could use the pattern revealed at 4:13.

If the fellowship is considering doing a series of midweek Bible studies on 1 Peter, a short amount of time giving an overview from the pulpit might help the Bible study group leaders and members to see how the main themes of the letter are developed. Alternatively, this format may lend itself naturally to a day conference where you want to get to grips with a particular book of the Bible.

Series 2. Five Sermons

Sermon 1	1:1-21
Sermon 2	1:22–2:10
Sermon 3	2:11–3:12
Sermon 4	3:13–4:11
Sermon 5	4:12–5:14

Developing from Series 1 above, sermon 1 focuses on the theme of hope (1:3, 21) and the future privileges of God's chosen people. Sermon 2 continues by focusing on the current privileges of God's chosen people. Sermon 3 builds from 2:11, 12 on Peter's strategy for living within the world as exiles, whilst sermon 4 enables the preacher to give more significant attention to the Christian response to opposition, seen mainly at 3:13–4:6. Sermon 5 concludes the series by giving an overview of Peter's final section. There are occasions when this is an appropriate length for a series, such as over a weekend. 1:1, 2 could also be used as a short 'taster' before embarking on the main teaching sessions.

Series 3. Eight Sermons

Sermon 1	1:1-12
Sermon 2	1:13-21
Sermon 3	1:22–2:10
Sermon 4	2:11-25
Sermon 5	3:1-12
Sermon 6	3:13–4:11
Sermon 7	4:12-19
Sermon 8	5:1-14

This series is an expansion of series 2 and gives more space and time to work through the letter. A series of this length might be suitable for a term of weekly Bible studies. Often the interruptions of other church events would mean that a series of eight sermons could be spread over several months. Given the way that 1 Peter is structured this series would make it possible for up to three different people to be involved in the preaching, with one preacher tackling each of the sections (1:1–2:10; 2:11–4:11 and 4:12–5:11). Each preacher could consider their own section of 1 Peter and also see how their sermons should connect with one another.

Series 4. Sixteen Sermons

Part 1

Sermon 1	1:1, 2; 5:12-14	A special people
Sermon 2	1:3-12	God's people have a glorious future
Sermon 3	1:13-21	Living as pilgrims on the way to glory
Sermon 4	1:22–2:3	God's people have a glorious new life
Sermon 5	2:4-10	God's people have been chosen for a glorious purpose

Part 2

Sermon 6	2:11, 12	A strategy for living as God's people in the world
Sermon 7	2:13-17	Living as God's people in the world
Sermon 8	2:18-25	Living as God's people in the workplace
Sermon 9	3:1-7	Living as God's people in the home
Sermon 10	3:8-12	Living as God's people in the church
Sermon 11	3:13-22	Confidence in Christ's victory
Sermon 12	4:1-6	Confidence in Christ's example
Sermon 13	4:7-11	Living as God's people in the light of the end

Part 3

Sermon 14	4:1-19	Suffering and glory in the world
Sermon 15	5:1-4	Suffering and glory in Christian leadership
Sermon 16	5:5-11	Suffering and glory in the church

This series is the selection developed within this book. As indicated above, it could easily be broken into three parts for three series given over the period of a year.

My own preference is to work through a longer series (even if it needs to be interrupted once or twice), as there are many benefits from dealing with 1 Peter in this way. Shorter series inevitably involve leaving out much helpful material. Furthermore, it is so important as an expositor to be sensitive to the genre and to seek to 'go with the flow' of the letter. A longer series gives you space and time to show how Peter's message fits together, whilst also giving time for explanation and application. It gives an opportunity for the preacher to deal with shorter passages which can provide an overview of the next section (e.g, sermons 1 and 6 in series 4), whilst also giving space to unpack longer passages.

Some thematic series, and thoughts on the part they can play alongside an expository approach, will be considered in the 'Other preaching possibilities' sections near the end of each chapter. But my advice would be that this is more safely done when the preacher has completed the hard graft of working through the whole letter. Only then will it be possible to guard against plucking texts out of context. A further chapter has been included specifically to help with a sermon on the person and work of Christ.

Structure of the chapters which follow

Each chapter within this book is based on a relatively short portion of 1 Peter and follows a consistent structure or methodology, specifically geared to help the preacher to get to grips with the text, in order to teach it. Some brief comments follow which will help explain how this process seeks to serve the purpose of proclaiming God's Word.

(1) *Listening to the text*
i) *Preliminary observations*
Careful attention to the text is critically important. What we think is there, or what our systematic theology informs us should be there, may not necessarily be present at all. An attempt has been made to look as sensitively as possible at the text in order to highlight significant words or themes as well as connections with other parts of Scripture. It is often useful to ask why a passage has been included or to consider the links with preceding and following passages. Finally, it is vital to see how each text forms part of the overall flow of 1 Peter. These preliminary observations are not meant to be exhaustive, but provide helpful insight which should be borne in mind before tackling the passage.

ii) *Exposition*
The intention here is not to produce a full, technical commentary on 1 Peter, but simply to give an explanation of how the text fits together so that the preacher can see

the main ideas within the passage. The titles and headings aim for clarity and are not chosen with the pulpit directly in mind.

(iii) Summary

A brief paragraph is included to try to draw together the various strands within each passage. The summary also seeks to highlight the way in which each individual passage contributes to the flow of the whole epistle.

(2) From text to teaching

By this point we should have got to grips with the essentials of the passage and now have a 'text to explain'. However, if that is the end point our sermon is likely to be presented like a lecture or commentary. To preach a passage we need to move from a 'text to explain' to having a 'message to proclaim'. To assist in this process a number of steps can be identified.

i) Get the message clear

The main concern here is to nail down the essential message of the text. A helpful way to do this is to identify the big idea or the main theme. We can then consider what main question(s) the text addresses. If our preaching is to be engaging then our sermons must answer questions, and these should be the questions addressed by the passage. It is good to state the big idea of the passage in one succinct sentence, and then to express this as a question. The preacher can go on to show why the big question is important and relevant for listeners.

ii) Engage the hearer
Point of contact

It is important to give careful attention to the introduction to a sermon. Rather than start immediately in the Bible, my preference is to start with ordinary life situations and then raise the issue to be addressed by the Bible passage.

Starting the sermon in this way provides a 'hook' so that people can immediately see that this sermon and Bible passage may have immediate relevance to their lives. A good introduction should therefore establish a point of contact with the listeners and connect with the big idea or the big question of the passage.

Dominant picture

Rightly handled, illustrations can provide windows within the structure of our sermons and bring light, clarity and understanding. My own general rule is that each point needs to be carefully illustrated and applied so that those listening can more easily understand what Peter is saying to them. However, illustrations often date quickly and may arise out of the preacher's own observations, reading, experiences and setting. I have tried to assist the preacher by providing one illustration which helps to explain and throw light on one of the central teaching points in the passage.

(3) Application

The purpose of including this section is as a reminder that 1 Peter contains a message which is to be preached so that lives are changed as a result. Of necessity the application is fairly general and would need to be sharpened up considerably for use in any given situation. Readers will see that each of the application points links to a teaching point made in the exposition earlier within the chapter.

(4) Proclaiming the message
i) A preaching outline
A title and preaching outline based on the exposition are suggested.

ii) Other preaching possibilities

This section is designed to assist in the process of deciding how to divide up 1 Peter. Various possibilities are suggested indicating where and how one passage can be linked with another. Also, although the assumption is that preachers will want to tackle 1 Peter in an expository fashion moving from passage to passage through the whole of the letter, from time to time themes are suggested which it might be profitable to explore.

iii) Leading a Bible study

The final part of each chapter includes a Bible study with some suggestions for questions which could be used by the leader. The Bible study works through four logical steps:

+ Introduce the issues – an opportunity to think about one of the main issues which will be raised by the text in order to engage the group members.
+ Study the passage – questions designed to help the group to dig into the text for themselves.
+ Think it through – questions designed to help members reflect on what they are discovering in the Bible passage.
+ Live it out – questions designed to sharpen the application of the lessons learned from God's Word.

(5) Peter – the model preacher

Before moving into the text of 1 Peter it is helpful to see that 1 Peter has much to say directly to the preacher. Peter is a model to guide us in the way we undertake our preaching ministry.

i) Expounding God's Word with conviction

Clearly Peter was an energetic and powerful preacher. Though regarded by the Jewish authorities as unschooled and ordinary (see Acts 4:13), his preaching was used by God in dramatic ways. Luke records for us edited highlights of his sermons at Acts 2:14-41; 3:12-26; 4:8-12; 5:29-32; 10:34-43 and 15:7-11. He is passionate about the Lord Jesus Christ and salvation through His cross and resurrection, now made available by God's grace to all, both Jew and Gentile. That same focus on the Lord Jesus Christ is very evident within his first epistle.

In both his Acts sermons and 1 Peter we see him constantly referring back to the Old Testament. This is God's Word which needs to be understood because of the light it sheds on the Lord Jesus Christ and the salvation now available. Though the coming of the Lord Jesus Christ has changed everything, Peter firmly bases his teaching on God's revealed Word given in the past, knowing that this is the foundation for God's unchanging purposes (see 1:10-12; 1:15, 16 etc.). Peter is clearly committed to expounding all of God's Word.

Furthermore, his understanding is that the Word he brings both from the Old Testament and now also revealed to him in these New Testament days is a living and enduring Word (see 1:23): 'living' because as it is preached God Himself (by His Spirit – see 1:12, 25) is at work bringing new birth and life (1:3, 23); 'enduring' because the results of this Word are permanent and last for all eternity (1:23-25).

Peter's conviction is that as the Word of God is preached the work of God is done and so his passion is to explain that Word and see it take root in the lives of his hearers. On the basis of his teaching at 4:11 he would have been only too aware that the preacher is one who is handling the very words of God. No doubt Peter would have embarked on every sermon with the desire that God's name rather than his own would be glorified in the process (see 4:11).

Confidence that what we are preaching to our people is the very Word of God is at the same time both an awesome responsibility and an amazing privilege. Taking our cue from 1 Peter we are to preach with passion and conviction.

ii) Expounding God's Word with illustration

In 1 Peter we also see how Peter constantly illustrates his material. Sometimes he uses a picture from the Old Testament; in 1:13 he wants his readers to see themselves as God's people emerging from Egypt 'preparing themselves for action' (lit. 'girding up their loins') in order to head towards the Promised Land. At other times he uses contrasts and comparisons to illustrate. For example he speaks of the value of Christ's sacrifice (1:18, 19) by referring to it as so much more valuable than the gold and silver that is exchanged at the local marketplace. Elsewhere he uses illustrations from the farm or garden (e.g. 1:23 – the seed) or from the home (e.g. 2:2 and the intimate picture of the baby feeding from the breast). They all help preachers to see the importance of illustrative material and give pointers to where such material can be gathered. Peter's teaching is neither dry nor academic; it is alive with pictures and images which enable us to appreciate and understand his message.

iii) Expounding God's Word with application

Peter is not interested in teaching for its own sake. His great desire is that believers know how to live an authentic Christian life amidst all the pressures of the pagan society which surrounds them. With that in mind he gives plenty of time to careful application, for example, highlighting the type of godly lifestyle he wants to see at 2:11, 12. He follows this with by a section showing how this lifestyle is to be worked out within society, at work and in the home (see 2:13–3:7). Careful and thoughtful application to the different groupings within our own church family needs to be modelled on Peter's approach. Furthermore it is evident within his application that Peter is sensitive to some of the awkward situations which many are facing. He is aware of intimidation in the workplace (2:19f) and of the frustration felt by the Christian wife about her unconverted husband (3:1ff). Peter understands his people and directs his teaching to them so that all can see the direct relevance of the Word of God to their everyday situations.

iv) Expounding God's Word with a love for people – compassion
Added to all this is a sensitivity to the real suffering which he knew many of his hearers would be facing. Aware of their suffering and persecution in its various forms, he gives careful application based on good theology (see 3:13-22 and 4:1-6), undergirded by a love for these fellow believers whom he regarded as his brothers and sisters (see 1:22; 2:17; 3:8; 4:8 and 5:9 for the theme of brotherly love). He addresses them as his 'dear friends' and as someone who has gone through the fires of persecution himself (see 5:1) he lovingly and sensitively encourages them not to be surprised at what they might need to go through (see 4:12ff), fully aware himself of what it might involve. This sympathetic and loving approach also applies to the local church leaders. Rather than flaunting his apostolic authority, Peter simply draws alongside as a fellow elder (5:1), seeking the same reward as them from the Chief Shepherd. His love for these people is a model for today's preacher. It should inform their preparation of sermons and their direct interaction with God's people from the pulpit and during informal conversations.

v) Expounding God's Word with a love for God – passion

Yet over and above his love for God's people, Peter reveals his passion for God. He begins with an outburst of praise for what God has done in Christ (1:3ff) and the second and third sections end in climaxes of praise of God (4:11 and 5:11). Peter is passionate about the God he serves and that passion is focused especially in his delight in everything which relates to the Lord Jesus Christ. As chapter 19 seeks to show, the whole letter is centred on the Lord Jesus Christ; the note of joy in the Lord Jesus both now and in eternity (see 1:6, 8; 4:13), seems to transfuse Peter's whole approach to living the Christian life. The way Peter communicates God's Word reveals a preacher on fire for God and the gospel, informed by a clear vision of glory to come and the prospect of seeing the Lord Jesus face to face.

Like Peter, we need to use the gifts God has given us faithfully (4:10, 11), confident that God's Word is living and enduring (1:23). We will want to use illustrative material as we carefully apply the Word so that in every way it is accessible. People will then be able to feed on it and will be strengthened in their pilgrimage to glory. All this must be done with both compassion for the flock and passion for the glory of the Lord Jesus Christ. Let us make sure that we ourselves have come under the influence of 1 Peter in the way we go about preaching it.

SECTION TWO:

Preaching a series

3

'A SPECIAL PEOPLE'

(1 PETER 1:1-2, 5:12-14)

Significant clues to the purpose of many books in the Bible can be discovered by taking a careful look at the opening and closing passages. The author will often want to establish the main themes at the outset, in a similar manner to a headline in a newspaper. 1 Peter is no exception and therefore it seems appropriate to bring together 1:1-2 with 5:12-14 for the first exposition. Not only does this give the preacher an opportunity to consider these verses on their own terms, but it also provides an overview for the whole letter which can be invaluable for the congregation as they start to see how it all fits together. What we will find is that 1:1, 2 set out the agenda for 1 Peter and give us a framework for his three sections (1:3–2:10; 2:11–4:11 and 4:12–5:11).

Listening to the text

(1) Preliminary observations

i) Every detail seems to be important in these opening verses. The fact that the letter is written by the apostle Peter alerts us to the fact that we should not be surprised by references to Jesus' ministry, e.g. 3:14; 4:13f; 5:1-4; 5:5 and 5:8 (see later chapters for more information on this). The language of some of Peter's sermons recorded in Acts will also appear, and the background of his own persecution informs his teaching to Christians under pressure.

ii) Peter writes to those described as the 'elect', who have been chosen by God (see also 2:9 and 5:13). Given that this theme occurs at the beginning and end of the letter it seems right to infer that it is a governing thought for Peter.

iii) Similarly, those who have been chosen are referred to as 'exiles' (ESV) or 'strangers' (NIV). See also 2:11. Those who have been chosen live as exiles or in exile, away from home. This links with Peter's own situation. At 5:13 Peter describes the chosen people as residing in Babylon. This is almost certainly a reference to Rome, yet Peter uses a code name to underline the fact that believers, wherever they live, are currently in exile.

iv) We need to let the text of Scripture surprise us rather than come to it assuming that we have all the answers. For example, we normally think of the Godhead in terms of Father, Son and Spirit, and other passages within the New Testament confirm this order (see Matt. 28:19). However, Peter uses the order Father, Spirit and Son (1:2). Peter probably wants to conclude with the believer's relationship with Jesus Christ. As we shall see, he thinks of conversion primarily as obedience to Jesus Christ (see 1:2, 14, 22) and the person who is not a Christian is in that position due to their unwillingness to obey (see 2:8; 3:1(ESV); 4:17). Obedience to Christ and conformity to his pattern of life will be a major factor within the letter, especially in section 3 (4:12–5:11)

(2) Exposition
i) Remember who you are (1:1)
a) You are the elect – chosen by God

Though the recipients of this letter are scattered on the far fringes of the Roman Empire, they are central to God's purposes and hold an extremely privileged position. Originally the phrase 'God's chosen people' was applied to the Israelites in the Old Testament (e.g. Isa. 43:20, 21) but now, through Peter's personal involvement, the door has been opened to include Gentile believers (see Acts 10, 11, 15). Though Peter had been personally selected and chosen by the Lord Jesus Christ (see Mark 3:13ff), every Gentile Christian can consider himself personally chosen by God.

Although there is some debate about whether the recipients were converted from a Gentile or Jewish background, the evidence of 1:14, 18 and 4:3ff leads most commentators to hold that they were Gentiles. Though formerly ignorant of God (1:14) and involved in a futile existence (1:18) these people are now standing in a privileged relationship with God.

Further, as God's chosen people, Peter's mind may well have gone back to the teaching he received from Jesus recorded in Mark 13:20-27. Amidst the struggles and persecutions which the church would go through before Christ's return, there is the assurance that the elect will be protected and one day gathered up even from the remotest corners of the earth to be with God.

In declaring to these Gentile believers that they are chosen by God, Peter wants to help them recognise the glorious privileges they have and their standing in relation to God. This will be unpacked in the first main section of the letter (1:3–2:10).

b) You are exiles scattered throughout the world

In the Old Testament God's people faced a lengthy period in exile a long way from their homeland. Many were taken to Babylon and had to live in a hostile environment where they were under pressure to conform to the surrounding pagan culture and where resistance could lead to severe suffering (e.g. Daniel). In Peter's day there was still a 'diaspora', with Jews scattered throughout the Roman Empire, away from the original land promised to them (see where the recipients of Peter's Pentecost sermon originated from – Acts 2:5-11).

Peter picks up this theme and applies it to the Christians scattered throughout modern-day Turkey, though what he says applies to Christians all around the world (see 5:9). They are to regard themselves like the Old Testament Jews in Babylon living in a hostile environment (see 5:13). They are not to regard Cappadocia or Bithynia as their home. As with the Old Testament believers, their true home lies elsewhere (e.g. Gen. 23:4 and Heb. 11:13).

Therefore, whilst they live as exiles away from home, the new diaspora of God scattered throughout the world, they are not to give their allegiance to the surrounding culture. Instead, their allegiance is to Christ, who will one day gather up His people and bring them home. So, in telling these Gentile believers to see themselves as exiles, Peter wants to help them recognise who they are in relation to the world and their surrounding culture. This is unpacked further in the second main section of his letter (2:11–4:11).

c) *The tension of living as God's elect in exile*

When we bring 'elect' and 'exiles' together there is a tension. Though belonging to God with a future home in glory, the believers are currently in exile surrounded by hostile forces. The very fact that they owe allegiance to God whilst in exile virtually guarantees that they will have to face times of suffering because of who they are and how they live. It is no surprise therefore that one of the main themes Peter develops – particularly in the third and final section of his letter (4:12–5:11) – is the reality of suffering because of allegiance to Christ.

Even within the opening verse of the epistle, then, we have an interpretative key which is going to help unlock the whole of the letter.

ii) *Remember whose you are (1:2)*

How is it that these people from a Gentile pagan background have become 'elect exiles'? Since they inherited the futile ways of their forefathers (1:18) something must have happened in order to give them a different inheritance. The answer lies in the fact that they now have another father – God the Father who has worked in them alongside the Spirit and the Christ – and they now belong to Him.

a) *You belong to the Father*

From the Greek word for 'foreknow' we get our word 'prognosis'. It is the word you would use when a doctor informs you of how your health is likely to progress following an operation or course of treatment. It speaks of a knowledge of the future. The word can be used to describe what will happen if the doctor is powerless to alter events, or when the doctor is actively intervening to bring about a particular outcome. It is in this latter sense that Peter uses this word to show God the Father's sovereign purposes and planning throughout history. Christ the Lamb was foreknown before the foundation of the world (1:19-20), because Jesus Christ's death on the cross was carefully planned from the very beginning. In the same way God the Father's foreknowledge of these Christians relates to His decision at the very beginning to choose them, set His love on them and bring them to glory (cf. Eph. 1:4). From eternity they have been known by God the Father and they belong to Him.

b) You belong to God the Spirit

It is almost certainly a mistake to think of sanctification as solely the process by which believers grow in holiness. To sanctify is to set something apart for exclusive use and is therefore generally used within the New Testament to refer to one aspect of God's work within the events which make up conversion (e.g. 1 Cor. 1:30, 6:11 ESV). It relates therefore to the work of the Spirit in setting someone apart so that they can belong to God in order to serve Him. These believers have been set apart by the Spirit so that they now belong to God and already constitute a 'holy nation' (see 2:9).

Elsewhere in 1 Peter the work of the Spirit is associated with the proclamation of the gospel (see 1:10-12) which in turn leads to new birth (see 1:23-25). The connection between the work of the Spirit and the believer's new birth is also seen elsewhere in the New Testament (e.g. John 3:3ff, Titus 3:5).

Finally, the reference to the Spirit links to His role of resting on the believer amidst suffering (see 4:14). Even when believers are set apart by unbelievers to be insulted and persecuted, the Spirit of glory and of God has set them apart as belonging to Him.

c) You belong to God the Son, Jesus Christ

The point of the work of God the Father and God the Spirit is to bring people to obedience to Jesus Christ. Conversion is depicted in many different ways within the New Testament and even within 1 Peter. Peter can speak of people being born again (1:3, 23), believing Christ (1:8, 2:7) or being called (1:15). However, Peter's main term is obedience. Someone becomes a Christian when they obey Christ or obey the Word of God (see 1:2, 14, 22; 2:8; and ESV 3:1). Clearly obedience to Christ is to be an ongoing experience, but it includes conversion and the initial recognition of the Lordship of Jesus Christ. The work of God the Father and God the Spirit is to bring the believer into a situation where they belong to God the Son.

Peter balances the human aspect of conversion with a reference to what Christ has done, which enables the believer to enter a relationship of obedience to Him. Conversion occurs as the believer is 'sprinkled with his blood' (1:2).

It is clear that there is an Old Testament reference behind this phrase, though commentators are less certain about which text is most prominent in Peter's mind. It could be Leviticus 4, where the sprinkling simply shows the forgiveness of sin available to the believer, or Exodus 12 where the sprinkling of blood on the doorposts on the night of the Passover signifies preservation from God's judgment. The most important link, however, is probably with Exodus 24 where Moses confirms the covenant between the Lord and His chosen people (Exod. 24:1-8). At the heart of this event the people promise to obey the word of the covenant and in response they are sprinkled with the blood of the covenant. Together the obedience and sprinkled blood demonstrate that these people constitute the forgiven, chosen people of the Lord. They show that a covenant has been established between the Lord and his people so that they now belong to each other. Following these events God's glory descends (Exod. 24:15-18) and will accompany them all the way to the Promised Land.

Given this background, Peter wants his converted Gentile audience to understand that they are in the same sort of situation as God's people in Exodus 24. Like them they have been taken out of their old home ('Egypt' – see 1:14, 18). They have now been constituted as God's chosen, covenant people (see 2:9, 10) through the blood sacrifice of Christ (1:19) and their obedient response (1:14, 22); they must now commence their pilgrimage through the wilderness to the Promised Land (see 1:13). As they travel, they will also know God's glory resting on them even amidst difficulties (see 4:14).

Therefore in 1:2 Peter undergirds his initial description of these people at 1:1 with a theological statement which shows how the whole Trinity, Father, Spirit and Son are involved in their election as God's people. This makes it a relationship which the hostile world around them cannot break. Together, Father, Spirit and Son have constituted them as God's chosen covenant people bound for a new Promised Land (developed in section 1), set them apart from those around them so that they now live as exiled strangers in a world with very different values (developed in section 2), and brought them to a situation where they obey Jesus Christ as Lord, conforming to the pattern and example of His life (developed in section 3). This has all happened as a result of God's abundant grace which has given them peace with God (1:2). Their task is to appreciate and not depart from this grace (5:12) so that they may continue to enjoy this peace (5:14).

(3) Summary

Though these scattered groups of Christians, facing considerable suffering and persecution, might have felt marginalised and forgotten, Peter reminds them from the outset who they are and to whom they belong. Through the work of God the Trinity, they have been chosen to live as exiles in this world until they reach their promised inheritance. This is who they are – God's chosen people. This is where they live – as exiles in a hostile world. This is how they live – by obeying the Lord Jesus Christ. Within God's sovereign, eternal purposes they are certainly not forgotten; they are a very special people, belonging to God, Father, Spirit and Son.

From text to teaching

(1) Get the message clear

Big idea (theme)

Peter starts his letter by highlighting the true identity of his recipients.

You are God's elect, belonging to Him.

Big questions (aim)

Preaching or teaching on this passage should answer the following questions:

+ Why does Peter start his letter in this way?
+ What factors make up our Christian identity?
+ What things are true of every Christian?

(2) Engage the hearer
Point of contact

There are many times when we feel forgotten, insignif-icant and marginalised. Things happen around us at work or in the family, but we feel left out and abandoned. It is easy to see how suffering, persecuted Christians could also feel like that today and in Peter's time. In other parts of the world God may be blessing His church richly but we seem to have been forgotten. How else can we explain such suffering and persecution? Peter's aim is to convince these Christians that whatever is happening they have not been forgotten.

Dominant picture

In the context of an enormous supermarket, the items placed in your shopping basket might seem insignificant. Nevertheless, out of all the items available they have been personally chosen by you in order to be bought and brought back to your home. So it is with these scattered, seemingly insignificant, persecuted Christians, who have been chosen by God. People who feel that they are on the margins of the Roman Empire and on the margins of God's purposes are actually standing at the very centre of God's plan.

(3) Application

The exposition has been focused on the question, 'what did it mean then?' Only once we have understood how it was to be received when it was written by Peter are we in a position to move on, as we must, in order to avoid our preaching merely becoming an exegetical study. The preacher must consider the message which this text brings from that time to the present, in order to apply it to his congregation. The following points follow on from the expository work set out above, but they are suggestive rather than exhaustive, in recognition that each congregation is different and faces its own particular issues which need addressing through the thoughtful application of God's Word to them by the preacher.

i) How we view ourselves can have far-reaching implications. Often we see ourselves through the eyes of the culture around us and, as a result we may think of ourselves as fairly ordinary people, no different from others. Or perhaps we may even view ourselves as weak, insignificant people, making no impact on the world. Further, especially if going through times of difficulty and suffering, we may think that God is not concerned about us and may even have forgotten us completely. The answer to each of these issues is to consider more carefully how God views us. He sees Christians, individually and corporately, as His chosen people whom He has carefully selected and brought into a relationship with Himself. We have been chosen by God and now we belong to Him! This is a truth which we must constantly impress upon ourselves and our congregations. In every situation we face we need to be reminded of God's perspective.

ii) One of the other temptations Christians face is to be far too much at home in this world. We do this by adopting the values of the surrounding culture and adapting our lifestyle to what we see around us, sometimes to avoid hostility from the non-Christian world which wants us to conform to its way of living. We need to be reminded to see ourselves as exiles. Though we live in this world and make an impact on it by the way we live (e.g. see 2:11, 12), it is not our home. People living temporarily in another country, though they may need to learn a different language and conform to certain laws, have their true home and allegiance elsewhere. So it is for Christians. We are meant to live differently and to have different values because ultimately we have a very different destination.

iii) Often we face disappointments in the Christian life through our own sinfulness which can lead to spiritual paralysis. 'It's all up to me ... and I'm useless.' Yet, though in 1 Peter we find plenty for the believer to do, Peter begins by reminding Christians of what God has done. He chose us for salvation through the blood of Christ before the foundation of the world (1:2, 20). Think of the long-term planning involved! By the Spirit He has set us apart as belonging to Him, so even when we fail to live a holy life as we should (1:15, 16) we still belong to a holy nation (2:9). Through the sprinkling of Christ's blood we are cleansed, forgiven and secure, so even when we stumble into sin, the once-and-for-all sacrifice of Christ (3:18), covers our sins and assures us of our acceptance before God. The whole Trinity has been involved in a plan which has been working itself out from before the very beginning of time to bring us to salvation! Our security and confidence as believers always needs to rest on what God has done, not on our own actions or failure in the Christian life.

iv) The purpose of God's great work is to bring us to obedience to Christ so that we will continue to follow Him day by day as Lord and Saviour. Once Peter had responded in obedience to Jesus' call (Mark 1:16-18) he spent his next years seeking to follow Him and receiving instruction by word and example about what a Christ-shaped life would entail (e.g. Mark 8:34-37). In the same way our role as Christians is chiefly to be found in following Christ, obeying His Word, copying His example and letting the pattern of His life (cross before resurrection) become more and more etched on our own lives as we travel to our destination. Obedience to Jesus Christ is not only therefore the authentic mark of conversion, but also of the whole Christian life. Knowing, understanding and treasuring the Word of Christ is vital to a life which demonstrates obedience to Christ and is pleasing to Him.

Proclaiming the message
A preaching outline
Title: **'A Special People'**
Texts: **1 Peter 1:1, 2; 5:12-14**
(1) Remember who you are (1:1)
  i)   You are the elect – chosen by God
  ii) You are exiles
  iii) The tension of living as God's elect in exile

(2) Remember whose you are (2)
  i)   You belong to God the Father
  ii) You belong to God the Spirit
  iii) You belong to God the Son

Other preaching possibilities
1 Peter is a great book from which to teach people the Old Testament. Peter constantly refers back to it in order to teach New Testament Christians how to live, not only with direct Old Testament quotations (e.g. 1:16; 1:24f; 2:6-8; 2:22; 3:10-12; 4:18 and 5:5) but also with many Old Testament allusions hidden on or just below the surface (e.g. 1:2 and Exod. 24; 1:19 and Exod. 12; 2:3 and Ps. 34; 2:9 and Exod. 19 etc.). This could form a short preaching series, giving further opportunity to explain the Old Testament

in order that your congregation can better appreciate what Peter is teaching in his letter:

(1) God's covenant in the Old Testament	Exodus 19:5, 6; 24:1-7	1 Peter 1:2; 2:9, 10
(2) Sacrifice in the Old Testament	Exodus 12; Isaiah 53	1 Peter 1:2, 19; 2:22-24
(3) Living as God's people in the Old Testament	Psalm 34	1 Peter 2:3; 3:10-12

Such a series may be helpful especially where knowledge of the Old Testament is limited or even non-existent, since for Peter it is an essential building block in the construction of his letter. One idea could be to run a short series like this in a midweek teaching slot whilst you focus on the exposition of 1 Peter in the Sunday sermon series.

For some preachers, constraints of time may mean that you are not able to include a separate sermon covering 1:1-2 with 5:12-14. If that is the case you may wish to incorporate some of this material into a sermon covering 1:1-5 or 1:1-12, perhaps by using part of the sermon introduction to set the scene for Peter's letter. Whatever you do, recognise that these verses are vitally important in 1 Peter. Peter is marking out the foundations on which he will build in the rest of his letter and therefore this teaching is vitally important.

Leading a Bible study
Title: 'A Special People'
Texts: 1 Peter 1:1-2, 5:12-14
(1) Introduce the issues
We need to get our bearings in order to understand where the Christian communities, referred to in verse 1, are located, and also to consider the suffering that they were

currently experiencing (see 1:6; 4:12). How do you imagine members of a small persecuted church on the edge of the Roman Empire would feel?

(2) Study the passages
i)   For this first study it would be useful to encourage the group to read the whole letter out loud in order to pick out the main themes. What do you think are Peter's main concerns?
ii) How are God's people described in verse 1 and why does Peter particularly choose these terms?
iii) In what different ways do the persons of the Trinity act and why does Peter draw attention to the work of the Trinity in this way?
iv) What is the significance of 'being sprinkled by Christ's blood' (see Exod. 24:1-8 for the Old Testament background)?
v)   What is the purpose of Peter's letter according to 5:12-14?

(3) Think it through
i)   In what sense should the doctrine of God's election (choosing us to belong to Him) be a source of great comfort?
ii) How is it helpful for Christians to see themselves as living in exile?
iii) Why does Peter not use the normal order for the Trinity of Father, Son and Spirit? What is the impact of the order Peter uses?

(4) Live it out
i)   What are the implications of studying these passages, both for us as individuals, and corporately as a church?

ii) How can we encourage each other to press outward from the fringe with the gospel?

iii) How will this affect our giving, our praying and how we live our lives?

iv) As a church, how do we identify the fringe and press beyond it with vigour and devotion?

v) Where is our fringe now?

4

'GOD'S PEOPLE HAVE
A GLORIOUS FUTURE'

(1 PETER 1:3-12)

Having described these Christians as God's chosen people living in exile, it is natural that Peter now wants to help them understand where their true home lies. In this passage there is a particular focus on the future destination towards which they are to travel. It is a 'living hope', also described as 'an inheritance' and 'the salvation ready to be revealed at the last time'. Peter also addresses one of the issues which caused him to write to them, namely their suffering. There is a two-way connection between the 'future inheritance' and present suffering. On the one hand, their suffering causes Peter to remind them of the one thing which persecution can never take away from believers, namely, their future inheritance; on the other hand, he shows how suffering is one of the means by which God strengthens the faith of believers on the journey to their inheritance. He finishes the passage by reminding them that, though they may feel insignificant and even marginalised, nevertheless as followers of Christ they are in an incredibly privileged position.

Listening to the text

(1) Context and structure

This section of Peter's letter (1:3–2:10) starts and ends with references to God's mercy, and is also connected with the preceding verses. In 1:1 Peter has written to the exiles who are far away from home and now he refers to their new home in the Promised Land (see 'inheritance' 1:4). Further, in 1:2, Peter has reminded them that Christians are the covenant people of God, with particular reference to Exodus 24, where the people of God are just about to set off on the road towards the Promised Land. So the natural theological flow from 1:1-2 is to focus on the Promised Land/inheritance. Indeed 'hope' is to be a dominant theme in this part of Peter's letter (see 1:3, 13, 21). God's people have a glorious future inheritance in view. This vision is to strengthen and encourage them amidst all the struggles that they face.

One of the important things to be aware of is that we are studying Peter, not Paul or other New Testament authors. Although they all bring us the inspired Word of God, nevertheless they have different perspectives and emphases, including the use of the same vocabulary but often in varying ways. In this passage, for example, it is interesting to note that 'salvation' is exclusively future and that the dominant note is confident hope, anticipating to the day of the revelation of Jesus Christ – a very different emphasis from Paul's focus on salvation in the present (e.g. Eph. 2:4-10). Together Peter and Paul combine to give us a very rich understanding of the gospel, but to gain the full benefit of all the New Testament writings it is important that 1 Peter is interpreted on its own terms.

Observing links with later passages reveals important themes and coherence within the letter as a whole. Peter starts this passage with reference to believers being 'born again' (1:3 ESV), as he does with a later passage (1:22, 23). With regard to the person of Christ, Peter often focuses on the resurrection (see 1:3, 21; 3:21) and in particular develops the theme of the 'revelation' of His glory (1:5, 7, 13, 4:13, 5:1, 4). Furthermore, the word 'glory' is also found at 1:7, 8, 11, 21, 24; 4:11, 13, 14; 5:1, 4, 10. Repetition certainly emphasises the importance of this theme. Similarly, 'trials' – and rejoicing amidst them – occurs at 1:6-8 and introduces Peter's last main section of the epistle at 4:12-13. Although Peter does not immediately develop the theme of Christian suffering, it is nevertheless an important subject which is to be more fully addressed later.

Another theme running through Peter's writing is the contrast between the perishable and the imperishable. What this world values supremely is gold, which Peter views as perishable (see 1:7, 18; 3:3, 4 (ESV)). On the other hand what God values (and therefore what the Christian should value) is imperishable. This includes the inheritance (1:4), faith (1:7), the blood of Christ (1:18-19), the Word of God (1:23), a gentle and quiet spirit (3:4) and the crown of glory (5:4). Preachers can often make their point more effectively by a way of contrast ('not this ... but that ...'), a device Peter consistently uses to drive home his point. Occasionally, within a run of consecutive expository preaching, it can be refreshing to follow a theme such as this through the letter in order to fully understand Peter's mindset.

Within 1:3-12 there is a fairly easy structure to be discerned. 1:3-5 and 1:6-9 both end with 'salvation'. The final paragraph, 1:10-12, starts with 'salvation'. Since 1:13 begins with 'therefore' it seems appropriate to handle 1:3-12 as one section with 1:10-12 as the conclusion and climax.

(2) Exposition
i) You have a glorious future inheritance which cannot be taken
  away from you (1:3-5)

The dominant thrust is the focus on the future inheritance ('living hope' 1:3, 'inheritance' 1:4, 'coming of the salvation' 1:5, 'when Jesus Christ is revealed' 1:7, 'the goal ... salvation of your souls' 1:9). This is the glorious truth which causes Peter to praise God at the start of the section when he says, 'Blessed be the God and Father of our Lord Jesus Christ!' (1:3 ESV).

In the context of the suffering which the churches were facing, this focus on their future inheritance is especially important. When an individual or a church suffers it usually means that things are being removed, whether that be a church building, a pastor's reputation, believers' liberty or even their lives. In such a context Peter reminds them of the one thing which can never be taken from them: their future inheritance.

a) How is this inheritance made available? (1:3)

The gift of this future Promised Land is made available through God's mercy and is therefore totally undeserved. The first step is that the Christian is born again or experiences a new birth (as in John 3:3), which opens up a new life and a new future which Peter calls a 'living hope' – (see also 1:13, 21). This is only made possible by the resurrection of Jesus Christ from the dead: as Jesus is raised to new resurrection life with glory to come (1:21) so the Christian is granted new life by being born again with the prospect of glory to come (1:5, 7, 9, 13). Throughout the letter these parallels are important.

Again, it needs to be noted that Peter's emphasis is different from that of other New Testament writers. John speaks of the necessity of being born again in order to see or enter the Kingdom of God (see John 3:3ff), with the focus on present salvation. Peter uses the language of new birth but retains a focus on the future.

b) What is this inheritance? (1:4-5)

The future to which the Christian can look forward with confidence is the equivalent of the Israelite hope of the Promised Land, as viewed from their time in Egypt (see Exod. 3:8). For New Testament believers it is a secure inheritance which 'can never perish, spoil or fade' (1:4), with echoes of Jesus' words concerning treasures in heaven (Matt. 6:19-21). Though other inheritances can be frittered away before they can be claimed, this one is absolutely secure and guaranteed. The inheritance to be received is 'salvation' (1:5, 9), which is linked to the revealing of Jesus Christ (1:7, 13) and seeing Him in all His glory.

Moreover, it is not just that this inheritance is kept for the believer (1:4), but the believer is also kept for it (1:5). There would be little point in promising a glorious inheritance if there was only a slim chance of the believer arriving at his destination to receive it. So Peter assures his readers, especially in the light of persecution and opposition, that God's power will shield them all the way to ensure that they make it. Peter uses the military metaphor to underline the security of the believer en route to heaven, and again we pick up echoes of God leading His people through the wilderness (Exod. 23:20), protecting them along the way.

c) When is this inheritance received? (1:5, 7, 9)

The inheritance is to be revealed 'in the last time' (1:5), which is linked to the day when Jesus Christ is revealed (1:7, 13). Peter views Jesus Christ as present but currently hidden (1:8), needing only to be revealed at the appropriate time. At that point, and not until that glorious day, Christians will have reached their goal and will receive the salvation of their souls (1:9).

We should note again how our life is dependent on the pattern of Jesus Christ's life. According to Peter what happens to Jesus Christ happens to us. This is true of Jesus' sufferings (see 2:21-23; 4:1), but for the moment we can see that if it is Jesus' resurrection which will grant new life, it is the appearing of Jesus Christ in glory which grants the believer glory (1:7). To that extent Peter's view of the Christian life is one of continually following the Lord Jesus Christ. He has blazed the trail to our inheritance and we follow Him to meet Him there.

No wonder the natural response of the believer is praise (1:3) and joy (1:6a). Indeed, Peter speaks of rejoicing with joy that is 'inexpressible' (1:8b). What a glorious future awaits every believer! Though currently in exile, homeless and perhaps suffering in a hostile environment, the Christian has the prospect of a home in glory and of seeing the Lord Jesus Christ face-to-face.

(ii) You may have sufferings on your journey as God strengthens your faith (1:6-9)

However great our future salvation, and wonderful though the revelation of Jesus Christ will be, currently we do not see Jesus (1:8). While Peter had seen Jesus in the flesh, that is not the experience of these believers in their far-flung parts of the Roman Empire. Since Jesus Christ and our future glory are out of sight, it means that progress can only be made by faith, trusting in what God has in store for us.

Naturally, then, Peter picks up the theme of the import-ance of faith in God (1:5, 7, 8). In passing, note Peter's surprising emphases. Whereas it is normal to speak of beginning the Christian life by faith in Jesus Christ and continuing by obeying His Word, for Peter, the Christian commences his new life by obedience to Jesus Christ (1:2, 14, 22) and continues by faith. Again, it is important for us to read what is in the text rather than constraining the text to fit our suppositions, derived from other parts of Scripture – or from inherited traditions which may not even be biblical at all.

Given the importance of faith for Christians as they head towards their unseen goal, it is not surprising that God may have to strengthen that faith during their journey (see 1:6). That is the theme which Peter now introduces in 1:6-9.

The period of our pilgrimage between the present and the goal is characterised as 'a little while' (1:6, 5:10). In this period there may be grief because of various trials (cf. 4:12). Yet Peter can see that there is a very clear purpose behind these trials. They are designed to refine and strengthen faith (1:6) so that it will be seen to be the genuine article (1:7), and result in praise, glory and honour being bestowed on the believer when Jesus Christ is finally revealed. The Last Day will reveal that faith in Jesus Christ was not misplaced and will make sense of the whole journey with all its trials and difficulties. So currently we love and trust Jesus Christ though we do not see Him (1:8), though one day we will see Him in all His glory. On that day we will obtain the goal of our faith which is the salvation of our souls (note 1:9 has a future reference, being tied to 1:5 and 1:7). The trials have the function of strengthening our faith and to that extent assist us and spur us on towards the goal of our journey. Though there is an understandable reticence in dealing with sensitive issues relating to suffering and why some believers go through such difficult times, nevertheless Peter is very clear in this particular context that God often uses trials as a necessary means to help us to get to our final destination.

(iii) You are in an incredibly privileged situation (1:10-12)
Though trials are designed to strengthen faith on the journey to glory, nevertheless suffering could also provoke a sense of dissatisfaction. So at this point Peter brings his argument to its conclusion and climax by highlighting the enormously privileged position of these suffering exiles.

a) The Old Testament prophets didn't understand ... (1:10, 11)
Peter argues that the Old Testament prophets didn't understand their own message fully at the time, neither recognising the complete identity of the Christ nor discerning when He would appear (1:10, 11) (e.g. see Dan. 12:8). None of the Old Testament prophets was fully aware that, for example, the identity of the Suffering Servant and the conquering Messiah was one and the same. Though they speak of the Christ's sufferings (e.g. Isa. 53) and His glories (e.g. Ps. 2) they didn't fully understand how it would all work out.

b) ... but you do understand (1:12)
By contrast, the Christian does understand these things. Through the work of the Holy Spirit sent from heaven, Christians can understand what the Old Testament prophets were speaking about. They are now able to appreciate the good news about the Lord Jesus Christ and how His sufferings and subsequent glories together provide them with a glorious salvation. Given that the 'glories to follow' include the appearing and glory of all those who follow Christ (see 1:5, 7), Peter makes clear that the people to whom he is writing are themselves caught up in what the Old Testament prophets foresaw,

and underlines this by repeating the word 'you' in this section. His first readers, though on the edge of the Roman Empire, are the focus of attention in God's plan. Old Testament prophets were preaching specifically to them (1:10-12a). They had been addressed by the Holy Spirit and by those who actually told them the good news of Jesus Christ (1:12). They are so privileged that even angels long to be in their shoes (1:12c)! Given the hints (1:3-5) that their experience is to follow the pattern of Jesus Christ's, Peter is able to show that their sufferings, like Jesus' sufferings, will be followed by subsequent glories. This pattern of the Christian experiencing suffering now to be followed by glory at the end will assume even greater significance for Peter in his final section (4:12–5:11).

While Peter shows here that the Old Testament was clearly written for Christians, and therefore quotes from it in various parts of his letter, our preaching emphasis in 1:10-12 is the flow of Peter's argument highlighting the incredibly privileged position in which the believer stands, compared even with prophets and angels.

(3) Summary

Though these Christians are suffering and under much pressure, they have been granted an incredible future. At the end of their journey they will receive a glorious inheritance at the revealing of the Lord Jesus Christ. Any discomfort along the way, which may of course be considerable, is due to God's desire to strengthen their faith so that they arrive at their destination. God's people are to recognise the wonderful privilege of their situation as they take in what God has in store for them!

From text to teaching

(1) Get the message clear

Big idea (theme)

Through Christ we have been given a glorious salvation in the future which cannot be taken away from us.

Big questions (aim)

Preaching or teaching on this passage should answer the following questions:

- What is the guarantee the Christian will get there?
- Why does God sometimes send suffering?
- Why was the Old Testament written and who was it written for?

(2) Engage the hearer

Point of contact

Being on the wrong end of a burglary is an unpleasant experience. Precious things are taken away and lost forever. Suffering is also an experience of having things taken away (e.g. health). Persecution reveals this in even starker form, where it might be a building confiscated, a pastor arrested, or life taken. In such a context it is extremely important to be reminded by Peter of that which can never be taken away from the Christian.

Dominant picture

An Olympic coach may put an athlete through all sorts of painful and gruelling trials in order to enable them to finish well on the great day and achieve their goal. God is so intent on getting us across the line that He strengthens us through sending trials. Further, as we watch an Olympic competitor we long to change places because we can see what an amazing thing it is to be in their position. So, prophets and angels long to be where we are as Christians.

(3) *Application*

This passage is extremely helpful in challenging our complacency. It is possible for us to be so caught up with things around us that we fail to look up to God and forward to glory to come. Conversely, it is possible for Christians to live in the past as they focus on their conversion and on 'the good old days'. Either way Peter's orientation towards a future salvation jolts us out of such complacency and directs us forwards and onwards. This teaching can therefore be a means of clarifying the whole direction, orientation and meaning of our lives.

The dominant note in 1:3-9 is the joy which flows from our living hope and secure inheritance. Our aim as preachers should be to enable our listeners to echo Peter's sentiments: 'Praise be to the God and Father of our Lord Jesus Christ!' He wants us to see what is in store for every believer – a glorious salvation when one day we receive our inheritance and see our Lord Jesus Christ. Our aim should be to explain the message of verses of 3-5 in such a way that the natural response of our listeners is to rejoice and to be filled with inexpressible joy (see verses 6, 8) as they consider this glorious salvation which is awaiting them.

Further, this passage provides some much-needed explanation for our current trials. Preaching on suffering and trials will always strike a chord within our congregations. Undoubtedly great sensitivity is needed, and this side of glory we are not in a position to give definitive answers to explain every difficulty that we pass through (as we learn from the Book of Job). Nevertheless Peter's teaching shows us that if faith in an unseen Christ and an unseen future is of the essence in the Christian life then it should not be surprising that God will strengthen that faith in order that we keep on moving towards our goal. Seen in that light, suffering is not an obstacle to our journey but a means of helping us proceed forward with greater purpose and intent. This will need to be sensitively applied to enable people to see some purpose in their sufferings and why God should permit them to go through all kinds of trials.

It is easy for us to become discouraged, especially in times of suffering, and so to wish that we were in a different situation. Yet Peter teaches us that in fact the Christian is in such an amazingly privileged situation that the angels long to be in our situation. Our aim in preaching from verses 10-12 is to show that whatever our situation, whether discouraged or feeling insignificant and marginalised, we are at the very centre of God's eternal purposes and that we can look forward to sharing Christ's glories.

Proclaiming the message

A preaching outline

Title: 'God's People Have A Glorious Future'

Text: **1 Peter 1:3-12**

(1) *You have a glorious future inheritance which cannot be taken away from you (1:3-5)*

  i) How is this inheritance made available (1:3)?

  ii) What is this inheritance (1:4, 5)?

  iii) When is this inheritance received (1:5)?

(2) *You may have sufferings on your journey as God strengthens your faith (1:6-9)*

(3) You are in an incredibly privileged situation (1:10-12)
   i)   Old Testament prophets didn't understand … (1:10, 11)
   ii) … but you do understand (1:12).

Other preaching possibilities
Clearly this is a very rich passage and naturally it would be possible to divide it into three separate sermons:

(1) Your future inheritance (1:3-5)
(2) Your current suffering (1:6-9)
(3) Your privileged situation (1:10-12)

This might form a mini-preaching series in its own right, perhaps incorporating 1:1-2 as a scene-setter for the opening sermon. It would be important to ensure that each sermon is clearly set within the flow of Peter's argument. The fewer verses that are selected for the preacher's text, the greater the danger of missing the wider context and narrative flow, and therefore the greater the need to set things clearly within Peter's development of these themes.

Leading a Bible study
Title: **'God's People Have A Glorious Future'**
Text: 1 Peter 1: 3-12

(1) Introduce the issues
This passage focuses on the future inheritance of God's people and the confidence that they can have in getting there. What views does our society have about heaven? How important does the prospect of heaven seem to most Christians?

(2) Study the passage
   i)   What are the things in this passage which cause Peter to be so excited that he begins, 'Praise be …'?

ii)   How has the new birth come about and what does it lead to (see verses 3-5)?

iii) What are the things which guarantee that we will receive our inheritance (see verses 4-5)?

iv)   According to Peter, what is the purpose behind some of the suffering and persecution which Christians undergo (vv. 6-7)?

v)   What is the goal of our faith and what will we see when we arrive at our goal (vv. 7-9)?

vi)   Identify the different characters or groups in verses 10-12 and examine how they relate to the believers to whom Peter was writing.

(3) *Think it through*

i)   Identify what relates to past, present and future in this passage. What perspective does that give you in your current trials?

ii)   How appropriate is it for Christians to be confident about their future salvation (vv. 3-5)?

iii) In your experience how have trials strengthened your faith (vv. 6-9)?

iv)   In verses 10-12 insert your own name or the name of your fellowship wherever you see the word 'you'. What impact does this have especially if you are feeling marginalised and forgotten?

(4) *Live it out*

i)   How will this passage encourage you to keep going in the Christian life even when you are suffering?

ii)   To what extent should Christians now share the excitement and joy which Peter reveals in this passage?

5

'Living As Pilgrims On The Way To Glory'

(1 Peter 1:13-21)

As already identified, the situation of these scattered churches in modern-day Turkey has parallels with that of the Israelites in the Old Testament. Having been set apart as God's chosen people they are given the inheritance of the Promised Land. Following the events of Passover night they are then set free to make their way through the wilderness to their destination. Echoes of this story are found in this passage from Peter. Like the Israelites, they find themselves set free from their previous way of life through the death of a lamb, and they too are now to make their way in a manner worthy of God as they proceed towards their inheritance. This Old Testament framework shapes and informs how New Testament Christians are to live amidst all the temptations and pressures which would draw them back to their old lifestyles.

Listening to the text

(1) Preliminary observations

i) 1:13 starts with 'therefore', indicating that a new section has started, though linked to the preceding one and developing from it.

ii) The subject of hope has already been introduced, though the word in 1:3 has an objective quality, and is virtually identical to the inheritance itself. In this section 'hope' (1:13, 21) is being used to denote confidence in God concerning the future.

iii) The word for 'conduct' in 1:15 is repeated in 1:17 and 1:18 (though this is obscured in both ESV and NIV). This word is significant for Peter, occurring a number of times in section 2 including at 2:12(ESV), a pivotal verse for the whole epistle.

iv) Peter comes to his first direct Old Testament quotation at verse 16, which is applied directly to his readers – not a surprise since he explains that the Spirit of Christ was at work through the writing of the Old Testament (1:11). Together with the strong allusion to the Passover lamb (1:19), this reveals how Peter uses the Old Testament as a framework to help his readers see how they are to live in their own situation.

(2) Exposition

i) Look forwards (1:13)

The inheritance (1:4, 5) which the believer will receive when Jesus Christ is revealed is described here as God's grace (cf. 1:10)– a wonderfully lavish expression of God's generosity. In the light of this, Peter encourages his readers to gird up or prepare their minds for action.

We should not lose sight of the background allusions within this phrase. Peter might have recalled the similar phrase from Jesus recorded in Luke 12:35 which comes in the context of the servants waiting for the return of their master. This certainly fits in with the theme of the need to act appropriately before Jesus Christ is revealed. However, an even clearer theological link is found in the instructions given to the Israelites for Passover night (Exod. 12:11), where they are told to gird up their loins in order to set off for the Promised Land (KJV). Given the parallels already identified with Passover, the Promised Land and the designation of believers as God's chosen people, this connection seems very appropriate.

Therefore, if verses 3-12 are true and map out their future destination, then believers cannot just stay where they are. Instead, they need to pay full attention to the journey towards this glorious destination. Get your mind in gear! Think it through carefully and consider what you need to do as you travel towards your Promised Land.

The reality of an impending future event, such as a work deadline, can have a sobering effect in reordering priorities in the present, and so it is no surprise that Peter adds in the phrase 'being sober minded' (ESV) (cf. 4:7). Peter wants to see believers shape their lives now in the light of the wonderful day in the future when Christ will appear.

ii) Look up (14-16)

The structure of this section is fairly straightforward:

    a) Don't look back to your old ways (1:14)

    b) God's character (holy) should shape your conduct (holiness) (1:15, 16)

As obedient children (cf. 1:2, 22) believers are no longer to be conformed to their old behaviour, which was fuelled by ignorance of God (1:14), implying that the majority of Peter's readers were from a Gentile background. The believers must travel forwards to their destination without a backward glance, leaving behind former behaviour.

As the Israelites were often tempted to return to Egypt, especially when going through trials in the wilderness, so too amidst their suffering (1:6) these Christians might feel tempted to go back to their previous lifestyle. However Peter clearly warns them that that is not an option. They are not to look back but rather look up to God and reflect His character in their conduct.

The motivation for a positive, holy lifestyle comes from the character of the God who accompanies the believers on their journey. The One who called them is holy and that is the lifestyle expected of those who travel with Him. Just as the Israelites were told to 'be holy for I am holy' (Lev. 11:45) after God brought them out of Egypt, so Peter's readers are to do the same. Rather than having their lives shaped by the world around, they are to look up and be shaped by God's holy, distinctive character. Their behaviour is to display His distinctive qualities which set Him apart from sinners. They are therefore to mirror His distinctive love, forgiveness, faithfulness, justice etc.

iii) Look back (17-21)

The structure here is the reverse of the previous passage:

a) God's character (judge) should shape your conduct (reverence/fear) (1:17)

b) Do look back to the ransom He provided (1:18-21)

Considering this passage with the previous verses, there is a focus in the central part (1:15-17) on how knowledge of God should shape Christian conduct. This is reinforced by the contrasting requirement not to look back to pre-conversion life (1:14), but instead to look back to the cross of Christ (1:18-20).

Within this overlapping central passage there is a further link between God who has 'called you' (1:15) and believers who are to 'call on Him' (1:17 ESV). He has spoken to them in the gospel message and they are to respond in prayer to a God who has revealed Himself as their Father.

Despite, however, this reference to God as Father, the more important point in Peter's mind is that the Father is the impartial judge. The two concepts of Father and Judge are in fact not far apart. A father has a responsibility for making just and fair decisions for his family, being an impartial arbiter and where necessary enforcing the administration of justice. Peter next considers the appropriate response from believers to their Father who is also their judge.

Within the Old Testament, and especially the Pentateuch, the natural response to the revelation of God in all His glory is one of reverence, awe and fear. The command to 'be holy as I am holy' is often linked to such a response (cf. Lev. 19:2, 14, 32; Exod. 20:20; Deut. 6:2; 10:12 etc.) Appropriate reverence for God (2:17, 3:2, 16), instead of fear of others (3:6, 14), in shaping Christian conduct is an important theme within 1 Peter.

Peter makes this point while also referring to his readers' context. Verse 17 includes a word similar in meaning to 'exile' or 'stranger' in 1:1 and both words are used at 2:11. It is a further encouragement for his readers not to live like those around them but to remember that they are on a pilgrimage to an inheritance under a God who is weighing up the conduct of every person in the world.

Further incentive to revere God comes from looking back to the cross of Christ. What was the price and cost of the ransom which set them free? It was not expensive gold or silver that was used to rescue them from the empty life that they once had (1:18). Instead they were ransomed by the precious blood of Christ (1:19). There is nothing more precious to God the Father than the blood of His own Son. Yet what was most precious to Him was freely given in order to provide deliverance and forgiveness to sinners.

The description of Christ as 'a lamb without blemish or defect' alludes to the requirements for the Passover lamb (Exod. 12:5) and highlights again how the Exodus shaped Peter's theology. The Israelites who left Egypt, having been saved from the Angel of Death because of the blood of an unblemished lamb, would surely have been supremely grateful for such provision and rescue from God's judgment. Similarly, Peter's readers are to ponder the fact that they also have been spared God's judgment through the deliberate selection by God, before the creation of the world, of the Lamb of God, the Lord Jesus Christ, specifically for them. He died and shed His blood to bring them release from their old life (1:18).

Imagine how grateful a young boy leaving Egypt on Passover night would be for the sacrificial lamb which had spared his life and granted him freedom. There would no doubt be a sense of awe and reverence that this God who had revealed His power that night in exercising judgment, was the same God who had provided a lamb to bring him deliverance. Peter connects the wonder of deliverance from judgment through the sacrificial death of the Lamb, Jesus Christ (1:19), with a response of awe and reverence as we journey as strangers through the wilderness to our inheritance in glory (1:17). In the flow of Peter's thought, we can see the contrast between these two passages within verses 14-21. Don't look back to your old lifestyle (14) but do look back to the cross (18-20).

This passage could have ended here, but Peter never leaves us with Christ's suffering or death. He always completes the picture to show Jesus' current position (cf. 2:25; 3:22). Though the Christian looks back to the cross in gratitude, nevertheless he also looks forward to his destination. One day he will see the One who is now raised and glorified and have a confident expectation ('hope') that God will bring that day about. In effect, Peter's argument comes full circle, returning to the theme of hope which began this passage (1:13).

(3) *Summary*

Christians are to start travelling towards their glorious destination. This is to be done as the believer looks forward to the day of Christ's appearing, up to God's holy character and back, not to his old lifestyle, but to the cross of Christ. This should produce a life where the believer learns to live in awe of this supremely generous God and reflect His character.

From text to teaching

(1) *Get the message clear*
Big idea (theme)

Christians have a glorious destination ahead of them, towards which we are to travel confidently in a way which honours God.

Big questions (aim)

Preaching or teaching on this passage should answer the following questions:

- What sort of progress should we be making in the Christian life?

- What sort of lifestyle should mark the Christian on the journey to his inheritance?
- How should the death of Christ help me to live a distinctively Christian life?

(2) *Engage the hearer*
Point of contact
Most of us go on journeys from time to time. Some of them can become quite wearisome as we endure the daily grind of commuting, perhaps dozing off on the way. By contrast, Peter wants Christians to be fully awake and alert as we are on a journey which will take us face to face with Jesus Christ.

Dominant picture
The future constantly affects the present. A holiday abroad next month requires preparation, whether by purchasing tickets, arranging currency or packing appropriate clothes. In the same way the future is to influence the present for Christians travelling to glory.

(3) *Application*
This passage impels us forward in our Christian lives. As Christians it is easy to be complacent, simply marking time and making little progress. Peter wants to see change, growth and action. There should be an urgency about what we do as we think about where we are headed. Especially in situations where we are wedded to values of the world around us (14, 18), we need this encouragement to push on distinctively as Christians. If you had just been released from Egypt at considerable cost where would you be going and how would you live?

The passage also encourages us to consider God's character. In a self-centred world it is easy for us to spend considerable time on how we look and how things affect us. As has often been said we need a 'Copernican Revolution' so that, rather than God orbiting around us, we see Him clearly at the very centre of all things. It will be vitally important therefore to help our listeners to focus and meditate as clearly as possible on God Himself, whose holiness is revealed in His distinctive character and is to be the measure of our lives as believers. The fact that He is a Father who judges and who has spared us through the amazingly costly sacrifice of His Son should lead us to fear Him. Peter clearly wants our conduct to be shaped by God's character rather than the world around us (1:14, 18).

We are also presented with the incalculable cost of Jesus' death for us. Over-familiarity with the fact that Christ died for us can be a dangerous thing, which leads to ingratitude and complacency. Peter's argument forces us to confront again how precious Jesus' blood is, and this can be the means of breathing new life into our Christian experience.

Proclaiming the message
A preaching outline
Title: 'Living As Pilgrims On The Way To Glory'
Text: **1 Peter 1: 13-21**
(1) Look forwards (1:13)
(2) Look up (1:14-16)
(3) Look back (1:17-21)

Other preaching possibilities
Since 'hope' occurs at 1:3, 13, 21, in a shorter series on 1 Peter you could preach 1:3-21 as one sermon. Inevitably

not all the details can be considered but the sermon could
fall into two parts:

(1) You have a glorious inheritance! (3-12)
(2) So ... let's get going to our destination (13-21)

Leading a Bible study
Title: 'Living As Pilgrims On The Way To Glory'
Text: 1 Peter 1: 13-21
(1) Introduce the issues
All of us live in a culture with enormous pressures to conform to its prevailing standards. Where do you feel those
pressures the most?

(2) Study the passage

  i)   How is verse 13 connected to verses 3-12?

  ii)   In what ways should 'hope' make an impact on our
         current Christian experience (see vv. 13, 21)?

  iii)   What is to be the more dominant 'pull' for the
         Christian (see vv. 14-16)?

  iv)   What does a life reflecting God's holiness look like
         (see Lev. 19:2 and the instructions in the rest of that
         chapter)?

  v)   Why should Christians fear God (see vv. 17-19)?

  vi)   How have believers been delivered from God's judge-
         ment (see vv. 18-20)?

  vii)   How can we get an idea of the cost of our salvation(see
         vv. 18-20)?

(3) Think it through

  i)   What are the things which distract you from your final
         destination? How does verse 13 help in practical terms?

ii) In what ways could you be more distinctive as a Christian within your society (vv. 14-16)?

iii) Consider how much God paid for your freedom. How should that affect the way you live (vv. 17-20)?

iv) Put yourself in the position of an Israelite escaping from Egypt after Passover night. What are the parallels between that experience and yours?

(4) *Live it out*

i) How will this passage encourage you to get going and live a more distinctively Christian life?

ii) The Christian life is lived out in recognition that one day (v. 13) we will meet the One who bled for us (v. 19). How should our gratitude and devotion to Christ be shown?

6

'GOD'S PEOPLE HAVE A
GLORIOUS NEW LIFE'

(1 PETER 1:22-2:3)

Peter's focus so far has been on the future, and the living hope which the gospel of Jesus Christ provides. However, at 1:22 there is a significant change in emphasis which can be observed in the following ways.

1:3-21	1:22–2:10
• Begins and ends with 'hope' 1:3, 21 • Imperishable inheritance at the end 1:4 • Focus on future privileges of God's chosen people • Message: this is what you will have	• Begins and ends with 'now' [NIV] 1:22; 2:10 •Focus on present privileges of God's chosen people. • Message: this is what you currently have- love for God's people–love for God's Word– love for God Himself.

Peter will soon describe the Christian's relationship with the world (2:11ff), but for the time being he is explaining the Christian's relationship with God. He moves from focusing on the future (1:3-12) and how you get there (1:13-21) to the present and how you live now. In 1:22–2:10 Peter highlights the marks of a believer in a vibrant relationship with the living God: a love for God's people (1:22; 2:1), for God's Word (1:23-25; 2:2, 3) and for God Himself (2:4-10).

79

Listening to the text

(1) Preliminary observations

i) Verse 22 seems to start a new unit within section 1 (1:3–2:10). Peter focuses on conversion both from God's angle (new birth) and our response (obedience – cf. 1:2, 14).

ii) Peter returns to the imperishable/perishable theme. Note again that what is imperishable cannot be taken away from Christians – whether it is their future inheritance (cf. 1:4, 18, 23) or their new life.

iii) Whilst considering Peter's teaching on its own terms, it is helpful to note parallels in this text with James 1:18-21.

iv) Peter has taught that Christians are in a similar position to the Israelites leaving Egypt and heading towards the Promised Land. Both Exodus and Numbers teach that the Israelites immediately faced disputes, grumbling and envy. Peter, therefore, now turns to address how believers should travel together. The 'you' in 1:3-21 is consistently plural, but in English this emphasis can be lost and so it is particularly helpful that Peter now unpacks the corporate implications.

v) There are a number of indications that 1:22-25 and 2:1-3 should be considered together:

    a) The 'therefore' at 2:1 clearly suggests a link.

    b) The command to love in 1:22 seems to be developed at 2:1.

    c) There is a continuing focus on the place of God's Word in the life of the Christian (1:23-25 and 2:2)

vi) The structure of this text reveals the following:

    A. How did you start the Christian life? (1:22a)

      B. The command: love one another (1:22b)

        C. Reason: you were born again through the Word of God (1:23-25)

      B. The command: love one another (2:1)

    A. How do you continue the Christian life? (2:2, 3)

In the exposition the central portion will provide the starting point from which the 'outer' layers will be developed.

(2) Exposition
i) God's Word preached brought new life (1:23-25)
New birth resulted from the resurrection of Jesus Christ (1:3) which revealed God's power to give life to the dead. However it is applied through the preaching of God's Word (cf. James 1:18) – an activity in which the Holy Spirit is intimately involved (1:12), and which has happened for Peter's readers (1:25) resulting in their new birth. As so often in Scripture (e.g. Eph. 6:17) Word and Spirit are held together – a word ministry is a Holy Spirit ministry and vice versa.

Peter's main point, however, is revealed in his description of God's Word as imperishable, supported by the Old Testament quotation from Isaiah 40:6-8 (1:24, 25a) and the description of the Word of God as not only living, but enduring or abiding (1:23). The work that God's Word has done is not something that is here today and gone tomorrow like the flowers in the field. Rather it has permanent and eternal consequences - an awesome consideration for those involved in the privilege of preaching God's Word. The lives of those around the Christian are based on ignorance (1:14) and characterised by futility and emptiness (1:18) and will ultimately wither away (1:24). By contrast, the Christian has been granted new birth into a life which is eternal and permanent.

It is worth reflecting again on the specific context of the churches to whom Peter was writing. Suffering and marginalised as they were, it would be easy for them to be impressed by the 'glory' and power of the secular authorities, including the emperor, and to think of their own lives as disposable when persecution took its toll. However, Peter wants them to look at things in an entirely different way. The 'glory' of Emperor Nero or local officials will soon fade away like the flowers in the field (1:24). By contrast, though they face persecution, their life is imperishable through the planting of God's Word in their lives which can never be extinguished by man.

But what sort of seed (1:23) has been planted within the Christian? A seed grows into a plant which will have a distinctive flower. What sort of flower should we expect to emerge from the seed that has given new birth to the believer?

(ii) New life is to be marked by love (1:22, 2:1)
It might be thought that if the seed is the Word of God, the flower would be knowledge of that Word. But the flower which Peter already sees emerging (1:22) and which he wishes to see grow fully is the flower of love, specifically brotherly love for other Christians (1:22). This can only occur as the truth is obeyed and as the soul is purified by the cleansing of Christ's blood. Both our obedience and Christ's cleansing are similarly mentioned at 1:2. That is the whole point of planting the seed, so Peter issues the command 'love one another deeply, from the heart' (1:22). If faith and hope (1:21) signify the invisible theological bonds which bind us to God and our future inheritance, love is the visible bond binding us to other believers as we journey together.

Peter uses a series of phrases which build up a picture of the church as God's family. God is Father (1:17) and through new birth (1:3, 23) believers become newborn babies (2:2) and obedient children (1:14) who are brothers and sisters (1:22; 2:17; 3:8; 5:9). Though the emphasis here is on brotherly love, nevertheless this wider theme is one that the preacher could develop separately if desired.

Brotherly love is to be pursued earnestly or deeply. The same word occurs again at 4:8 and has the meaning 'at full stretch'. The idea is of someone extending themselves further than they had done previously in order to demonstrate such love within the fellowship.

Peter then helps us to understand what that love entails by highlighting what needs to be removed from the life of the believer (2:1). The Christian is to put away or get rid of five particular items, all of which can disrupt relationships. The same word is used at James 1:21 with the idea of getting rid of weeds, which can hinder the growth of the seed planted within the soul. These sorts of activities (malice, deceit, hypocrisy, envy, slander) are like weeds and they must be removed. Only as they are weeded out will the full flowering of brotherly love within the church family be evident.

(iii) New life is to be marked by growth – through feeding on God's Word (1:22, 2:2, 3)

Love and Christian maturity grow as the plant is watered by God's Word. Here Peter changes to the metaphor of the newborn baby (2:2), although he uses it in a slightly different way from Paul (1 Cor. 3:1, 2) or the author to the Hebrews (Heb. 5:12-14). In those cases immature Christians are infants requiring milk, and the hope is that believers will mature and feed on more appropriate food for an adult. By contrast, Peter views each Christian as a newborn baby requiring milk in order to grow up as they continue on the road to salvation.

Christians start their new life through obedience to the truth (1:22), when they taste that the Lord is good (2:3).

They continue in the Christian life in exactly the same manner by feeding on His Word (pure spiritual milk) taking it in as an infant drinks in its mother's milk. Feeding regularly and growing physically are signs of healthy life in a newborn baby. Similarly, feeding regularly on God's Word and growing spiritually are signs of a healthy life in a believer.

The responsibility of the preacher is to provide spiritual milk which is pure and unadulterated. It must not be contaminated by false teaching or tampered with in any way. God's Word is the dynamic means of implanting life and of sustaining and developing life which flowers into a love for one another. The mark of real spiritual life, and the means of developing Christian character and brotherly love, will be a craving for this food.

(3) Summary
The Word of God planted in Christians has given them new life which cannot be taken away. This new life will be evidenced in love for God's people and for God's Word. Believers must undertake the journey to their glorious destination together and will require constant nourishment on the Word of God, in order to live as the people of God by loving one another.

From text to teaching
(1) Get the message clear
Big idea (theme)
Christians have been given a glorious new life through God's living and enduring Word, which should result in loving relationships within God's people.

Big questions (aim)

Preaching or teaching on this passage should answer the following questions:

+ How does someone become a Christian? What is God's role and what is our role?
+ What is the significance of the Word of God for the believer ... and for the church?
+ What sort of behaviour should be expected within God's family?
+ How can Christian life be sustained and developed?

(2) *Engage the hearer*

Point of contact

An old-fashioned steam engine needs to be stoked with fuel (input) in order for the train to move forward (output). In the Christian life if there is no input from God's Word then it is no surprise if there is no progress. Similarly, if there is no output in terms of greater love then something has gone badly wrong.

Dominant picture

In a garden a seed is sown which has life inherent within it: no seed, no flower. Once the seed has germinated it begins to grow until it is visible above the soil. It needs watering to enable it to continue to grow to its full potential and will benefit from the removal of weeds which would restrict and hamper its growth. Each aspect of this illustration can be seen in Peter's argument as he longs for the flourishing of Christian love within the church as they travel together to glory.

(3) *Application*

i) Only the Word of God through the Spirit of God can produce new birth and spiritual life. Though there may be many attractive things for the church to be engaged in, the priority must be to preach God's Word praying that God's Spirit will do His work by planting it in the hearts of those who hear. Further, the Word of God, read, studied or preached, is essential for the growth and well-being of the Christian community as it travels to its glorious destination. God's Word is essential for non-Christians and Christians and must therefore be given priority in the life, gatherings and outreach of God's people. To neglect the ministry of God's Word, either deliberately or by letting other ministries squeeze it out, is a recipe for losing any evangelistic cutting edge and producing weak Christians who will be at odds with each other.

ii) Only the resulting ministry from God's Word preached will prove to be imperishable and eternal. The church must view all its work and witness in the light of eternity and seek to focus on results which will be permanent – another encouragement for the church to give priority to the ministry of God's Word.

iii) We constantly need to be challenged in our love for one another. It is so easy for us to fail to make progress in this area and allow the various weeds of 2:1 to stifle growth. This passage searches our hearts, convicts us and should encourage us all to stretch further in loving one another in whatever ways are possible, such as time, money, effort or thoughtful actions. We dare not apply the importance of being a people committed to the Word of God without being committed to the people of God. Truth and love are not to be played off against each other but are both non-negotiable elements within the life of the Christian.

iv) Finally, there should be an encouragement for people to feed on God's Word – indeed to crave it. We must ensure that all possible assistance is provided within the church family to ensure that those who crave pure spiritual milk can be fed. Perhaps this means encouraging daily Bible reading or setting up Bible study groups or suggesting appropriate Christian literature to help people feed on God's Word. As preachers, we must model an appetite for God's Word and shape our ministries so that the flock can be fed (see 5:2).

Proclaiming the message
A preaching outline
Title: **'God's People Have A Glorious New Life'**
Text: **1 Peter 1:22–2:3**
(1) God's Word preached brought new life (1:23-25)
(2) New life is to be marked by love (1:22, 2:1)
(3) New life is to be marked by growth – through feeding on
      God's Word (1:22 2:2, 3)

Other preaching possibilities
This text would make a particularly appropriate study in enabling a church to consider its priorities, since it helpfully focuses on the Word of God and the people of God. Congregations and leadership teams may find this passage particularly helpful to clarify their tasks of evangelism and the nurture of disciples.

Picking up the link of 'born again' and 'imperishable' at 1:3ff. and 1:23, you might wish to develop a short series within section 1 (1:3–2:10):
(1) The new birth and a glorious future (1:3-21)
(2) The new birth and a glorious new life (1:22–2:10)
Another possibility, remembering to keep the connection with the rest of the letter, is:

(1) How do you start the Christian life? (1:22-25)
  i)   Obey the Word (1:22)
  ii) Receive the Word (1:23-25)
(2) How do you grow in the Christian life? (2:1-3)
  i)   Obey the Word (2:1)
  ii) Receive the Word (2:2, 3)

Leading a Bible study
Title: 'God's People Have A Glorious New Life'
Text: 1 Peter 1:22–2:3
(1) Introduce the issues
A seed ought to grow and a newborn baby should also grow, given the right nourishment. What are the reasons why we seem to find it easy to stop growing in the Christian life?

(2) Study the passage
  i)   What has happened to the believers in verse 22 and what is Peter looking for in their life together?
  ii) How does verse 22 relate to verses 23-25?
  iii) What are the main characteristics of God's Word revealed in verses 23-25 and why do you think Peter draws attention to them?
  iv) What is added by including the Old Testament quotation in verses 23-25?
  v)   What hinders growth in the Christian life and how should the believer respond (see 2:1)?
  vi) What do you think 'pure spiritual milk' is, in the context of 1:22–2:3?
  vii) What promotes growth in the Christian life and how should the believer respond (see 2:2, 3)?

(3) *Think it through*

i) What could loving one another 'at full stretch' mean in your situation (see 1:22 and 2:1)?

ii) What is the relationship between the Spirit of God and Word of God (see 1:12, 23-25)?

iii) How should verses 23-25 affect the priorities of a local church?

iv) What are the different ways in which we can encourage each other to feed on God's Word (see 2:2, 3)?

(4) *Live it out*

i) How will this passage encourage you to make progress once again in your Christian life?

ii) How can we encourage each other to love one another 'at full stretch'?

7

'GOD'S PEOPLE HAVE BEEN CHOSEN FOR A GLORIOUS PURPOSE'

(1 PETER 2:4-10)

This passage brings Peter's first section (1:3–2:10) to a climax and conclusion. Addressing the relationship Christians have with God through the gospel, Peter started at 1:3ff with a clear future orientation; he now finishes this section by focusing on the present and the privileges which the Christian already possesses (2:10), which are accessed day by day in coming to Jesus Christ (2:4).

This passage also clearly presents the purpose for which the Christian lives. Peter's teaching here is wonderfully God-centred. We are lifted out of our tiny man-centred plans and hopes in order to be given a tremendous vision of how we are to live our lives in a way acceptable to God. Believers have been chosen by God so that they can declare God's praises and delight in His goodness (2:9). If our ultimate goal (1:9) is to stand before the Lord Jesus Christ in glory, our current purpose is to delight in God for who He is and all His mercies shown to us in the gospel.

Listening to the text

(1) Preliminary observations

i) A key word within the passage is 'chosen'. Jesus Christ is twice referred to as 'chosen and precious'(2:4, 6). Similarly believers are 'chosen' (2:9 cf. 1:2) which further develops the parallel between Christ and the believer (note also that both Christ and the believer are described as 'living stones' in verses 4 and 5). If Jesus Christ is 'chosen and precious', then the believer stands in a similar relationship to God – a view reinforced by the avalanche of terms used at 2:9, 10. Meanwhile, Jesus Christ is chosen by God, though rejected by some to their detriment. Peter is perhaps suggesting that, if believers are also chosen by God, then their rejection by men will also be to the detriment of those who reject them (see 2:12; 3:16; 4:4-6).

ii) Clearly this passage is particularly rich in Old Testament quotations and allusions. The quotations in verses 6 to 8 from Isaiah 28:16, Psalm 118:22 and Isaiah 8:14 are all linked to the reference to 'stone'. However, there are also very strong Old Testament allusions at 2:5, 9, 10 with Peter particularly depending on Exodus 19:5, 6, Isaiah 43:21 and Hosea 2:23.

iii) Verse 4 appears to link coming to Jesus with 2:2, 3 and the experience of tasting that the Lord is good through His Word. The believer comes to Jesus at the start through obeying God's Word and day by day through feeding on God's Word.

iv) Translations differ at the start of verse 7. The esv has 'So the honour (presumably of being part of this temple built on Christ) is for you who believe' and is probably preferable. The Greek word means 'honour' and links to the honour Christians receive when Jesus is revealed (1:7).

v) The dominant theme of Section 1 has been that God's chosen people have a glorious inheritance towards which they proceed. The section ends by reinforcing the privilege of their current situation. Already they are God's chosen people! Once again we see Peter's readers in a comparable position to that of Israel after the Exodus. The Israelites were gathered together having been released from slavery in Egypt by God. They had the prospect of the Promised Land in view but Exodus 19:5, 6 shows the Lord reminding them of their amazing current status as His treasured possession. This same privilege is stressed within the flow of 1 Peter.

One way of looking at this passage is as follows:

A. Jesus Christ – living stone (chosen and precious) – whom some reject (4)

B. Christians – temple/priesthood/sacrifices (5)

A. Jesus Christ – living stone (chosen and precious) – whom some reject (6-8)

B. Christians – people/priesthood/proclaiming etc. (9, 10)

This would indicate that 2:6-10 is unpacking and developing, through Old Testament quotation and allusion, what is already referred to in 2:4, 5. Furthermore, the turning points within the structure highlight the position of Christ and the Christian in contrast with the non-Christian. For example, at the end of verse 4, though Christ is rejected by men, nevertheless God regards Him as chosen and precious, and verses 8 and 9 refer to those destined to stumble, and contrasting them with believers who receive enormous privileges.

(2) Exposition
i) A new temple (2:4-8)

The emphasis in this passage is on what God has done and is doing. Rather than focus entirely on what we as God's people have received at 2:9, 10 it is important to retain a God-centred approach. Just as God is the One who has granted new birth and an eternal inheritance (1:3, 4), so God is the One who is currently building a people for Himself.

His first act has been to lay a foundation stone for the building, which is how a cornerstone functions. This cornerstone is, of course, the Lord Jesus Christ who is chosen and precious in God's sight. This stone was rejected by some of the builders, which links to Jesus' parable of the tenants (Mark 12:10), where He uses the same Old Testament text (Ps. 118:22) as a prophecy of His death. However, as is so often the case in 1 Peter, the author wants to stress that Christ did not remain dead – hence He is the 'living stone' (2:4) as testimony to His resurrection.

On this living stone, the crucified and resurrected Jesus Christ, God is now building His house (2:5). This 'spiritual house' in which God dwells, where priests offer sacrifices, is clearly a reference to a temple which is built as believers come to Jesus Christ (2:4) and trust in Him (2:6, 7a). In this house/temple metaphor, believers are 'living stones' (2:5) because they, like Jesus, have been granted new life (1:3).

The emphasis here is that God is the One doing the building work ('you ... are being built' 2:5), which links with similar teaching in Ephesians 2:19-22 and the statement of Jesus Christ, 'I will build my church' (Matt. 16:18) which was specifically said to Peter.

The flipside of this emphasis is that not only will the efforts of men have no lasting detrimental effect on the construction of this temple, but also those who reject Christ will 'stumble' (used twice in 2:8). This is a result of not believing in Jesus (contrasted with those who do believe in 2:6, 7), and Peter describes this rejection as 'disobeying the message' (2:8). This fits with his earlier emphasis on conversion as a matter of obeying the Word (1:2, 14, 22). Clearly, for Peter, disobeying God's Word and not trusting in Jesus Christ amount to the same thing. Yet either way such behaviour does not derail God's eternal plan (cf. 1:2, 20) as 2:8b makes clear. Those who do not obey were destined for stumbling and (implicit in 2:6) shame (cf. 3:16).

This reminder of God's sovereignty over all things will be an important background factor when Peter starts to speak of how Christians are to function within a hostile world, where they will undergo suffering (2:11ff). Such experiences will demonstrate not that God's plans have failed, but rather how such behaviour fits in with God's eternal design. Some are appointed or destined to honour (2:7 ESV), whereas others are appointed to shame (2:6, 8). As people respond, either in faith and obedience to God's Word or in disobedience, so God's eternal plan is being revealed. God is building a temple and whether we are to be part of it depends upon how we respond to Christ, the living stone.

What an impact this passage would have had on these Gentile converts on the edge of the Roman Empire! Unlike their pagan or Jewish friends they had no temple to attend, either locally or in Jerusalem. Surely the temptation was to consider their newfound religion as in some way second class. Yet here is the reminder that they do have a temple in which to meet with the living God, made up of believers in Jesus Christ. As they met together in their local gatherings they formed the temple where God dwelt.

Furthermore, as a suffering marginalised group it would be easy for Christians to be tempted to feel ashamed about their faith in Jesus Christ. Later passages within 1 Peter speak of the verbal abuse suffered by Christians (e.g. 3:16). People might have taunted Christians about the stupidity of trusting Jesus – a mere man who had been executed by the Roman authorities. Yet this passage shows that ultimately it is believers who will be vindicated: their action of trusting Jesus will be shown to be the right action so that they need never feel ashamed.

ii) A new identity (2:5, 9)

As mentioned earlier, verses 4 and 5 set out the teaching which is unpacked in verses 6-10. Verse 5 highlights both who Christians are and also what they are to do within the temple. Both these themes are developed in verses 9, 10.

Four titles for believers are used in this passage. Not surprisingly, since the action takes place within this new temple which God is building, the designation 'priesthood' occurs twice (5, 9). Christians together form a holy and royal priesthood. It is not that some of them are in some sort of special priestly category whilst others are ordinary believers. Instead all Christians are a priesthood with particular responsibilities in view which will be explored later.

In verse 9 'priesthood' is joined by other titles largely taken from Exodus 19:5, 6. These Christians are not only a chosen people and a royal priesthood, but are regarded as a holy or set apart nation. This links with 1:2 since the specific ministry of the Spirit is to set people apart as belonging to God. They are also a people for His possession or a people belonging to God, echoing Exodus 19:5 'out of all nations you will be my treasured possession'. Given that Peter is about to set the life of the believing community within the context of the pagan Gentile world (2:12), Exodus 19 is a particularly important allusion. Before launching into the world, in both the Old and New Testaments, God's people are powerfully reminded of who they are and to whom they belong. In these four short phrases Peter reminds them with short hammer blows of the way in which God views them and how they should view themselves.

In a sense each of these phrases is simply unpacking what it means to be chosen by God – the overarching theme set out at 1:1. To be chosen by God whilst others are not (2:8) means that believers belong to God (a people for His possession). They have been set apart and marked out as different within the world through their beliefs and behaviour (holy nation), and have a specific purpose: to offer sacrifices (royal priesthood).

The shocking reality at the heart of this verse is that all these titles which once belonged to the Israelites have now been applied to these small gatherings on the fringes of the Roman Empire. Though perhaps regarded with contempt by their non-Christian neighbours (eg. 2:12, 15; 3:15) who are saying 'you don't belong', these titles reveal that they are regarded by God the Father as He would regard His own Son, chosen and precious to Him (2:4, 6, 9) – 'you belong to me'! What these Christians will receive in the future is incredibly impressive (see 1:3ff), but what they have already received from God is equally exciting and something for us to ponder carefully in order to encourage and strengthen us in all the struggles we face.

iii) A new purpose (2:9, 10)

It seems that the chief designation of God's chosen people, built into a temple of living stones, is that of priesthood, since it is mentioned twice in verses 5 and 9. According to verse 5, the role of such a priesthood is to offer sacrifices, which Peter clarifies as spiritual, acceptable to God through the work of Jesus Christ. In itself verse 5 does not explain further what Peter has in mind.

However, just as verses 6-8 explain what is set out in verses 4 and 5a, so it is appropriate to expect something in verses 9 and 10 to explain the second part of verse 5. The spiritual sacrifices Peter has in view are those of 'declaring God's praises' or 'proclaiming His excellencies' (ESV)(cf. Heb. 13:15). This picks up on a theme found in Isaiah 43:21 where the Israelites are 'my chosen, the people I formed for myself that they may proclaim my praise'. Part of the very purpose of being chosen by God is that there should be a natural response of praise, delight and joy.

This is underlined by Peter in the rest of verses 9 and 10. God's people will naturally want to declare His praise because of what God has done for them in Jesus Christ. In the gospel God has called them from darkness (cf. ignorance 1:14; emptiness and futility 1:18) into His wonderful light (which may refer to future glory (1:7) but since verse 10 refers to present realities probably refers to current experience). Furthermore, though at one time they were not part of God's people and had not received mercy, now, in words from the prophet Hosea, they are the people of God and have received mercy: they have a special status in God's eyes through being recipients of His undeserved love.

The words in Hosea originally referred to the exiles from the northern kingdom of Israel, although both Paul (see Rom. 9:25, 26) and Peter reapply them to the gathering in of believers from the Gentiles. From this point on, Peter will leave the Exodus narrative behind in his Old Testament references, and focus on other areas, quoting in particular from Psalms and Proverbs to show how God's people are to live within a hostile world. This is set up by the references in 2:10 which, coming from Hosea, point forward to the restoration of those in exile. Already, in terms of their relationship with God, they are restored, though the period of their exile will continue until the revelation of the Lord Jesus Christ.

The main thrust of these verses, however, is that given their current experience of God's mercy, they should celebrate God's goodness by declaring His excellencies, or as we might say, singing His praises. There has been debate as to whether this is a specifically evangelistic activity which takes place in the world, or an activity linked to the gatherings of Christians in their meeting places. Although it may be unwise to be too dogmatic, John Dickson in his book *Promoting the Gospel* (Good Book Company 2005) makes a good case for understanding the phrase to refer primarily to what went on as Christians met together. The word for 'declare' is a word apparently used often in a liturgical setting. Further, 'declare the praises' is a phrase which is always linked to what is said of the Lord in public gatherings of His people.

Dickson shows that such praise may often have a powerful effect on any unbelievers who are present as they overhear declarations about God's goodness in the gospel. Though the activity to which Peter refers is not specifically preaching the gospel (Peter would have used a different word), nevertheless it has a powerful effect in promoting the gospel. This also links with the next section which is designed to equip Christians to live in a non-Christian environment in a manner which promotes the gospel and leads to others glorifying God (2:12).

Peter brings this section to its climax by giving the answer to why God has acted as He has to provide salvation for His people. What is the reason behind the provision of the Lamb of God and the gathering of His chosen people? The answer lies in the fact that the purpose of our life as believers is to declare God's excellencies. Peter does not want these Christians to live for themselves or have small worldly ambitions. Instead he wants to lift their eyes to the reason for their existence as believers, which is to delight in God and bring glory to His name. It is a profoundly God-centred vision which directs them upwards (towards God) and outwards (enabling the world to overhear how good God is). This is to be the present purpose and privilege of the church.

(3) Summary

God has a secure inheritance prepared for His people in the future, but the believer already has much in which to rejoice. God is at work building His church as people come to put their trust in Jesus Christ. These people stand in an incredibly close relationship to God, belonging to Him. Having received so much from God through Christ already, the whole purpose of the life of the Christian is to bring glory to God's name.

From text to teaching

(1) Get the message clear

Big idea (theme)

Christians have a wonderful new identity and have been given a glorious new purpose as part of the present privileges of being God's people.

Big questions (aim)
Preaching or teaching on this passage should answer the following questions:

+ What is the significance of Jesus for believers and unbelievers?
+ What is God building and how does He do it?
+ How are God's people viewed by God?
+ What is God's purpose for your life?

(2) *Engage the hearer*
Point of contact
It is easy to get us talking about something which excites us. It may be a favourite football team or TV programme, or perhaps the latest gadget or fashion accessory, or a fiancé(e) or grandchild. Whatever it is, we have no difficulty speaking with delight and commendation and the very act of speaking adds to our appreciation. Peter wants us to appreciate God's goodness to us in the gospel so that we would have a similar desire to sing His praises.

Dominant picture
A child sees her favourite cuddly toy moved by a guest. Immediately she runs over and picks it up, clutching it to her and informing those around, 'that's mine!' God has a similar passion for His people whom He has rescued so that they find their identity in belonging to Him.

(3) *Application*
i) This passage highlights God's sovereignty. He builds His temple, He chooses His people and His plans are not affected by people disobeying His Word. Especially when the church is small and feels weak amidst powerful forces at

work within the world, this is a truth that needs reinforcing. God is building His church.

ii) The passage could certainly be used evangelistically. Verses 4-8 show Jesus Christ as:

- ✦ The rejected stone (pointing to the crucifixion).
- ✦ The living stone (pointing towards the resurrection).
- ✦ The cornerstone – the indispensable part of the house which God is building for Himself and His people.

In this light our response to Him is vital. Either we will listen, obey and put our trust in Him and receive honour and a place within the fabric of God's purposes; or, alternatively, we will disobey God's Word and find ourselves stumbling irretrievably and on the Last Day be put to shame. Jesus Christ is either the foundation stone of our lives or the stumbling block.

iii) In these days many people appear to suffer from low self-esteem. Collectively this should never be true of the church. Each of the wonderful titles for the church in this passage needs to be carefully considered, so that Christians can see how God views us and so how, corporately, we should view ourselves. Though perhaps weak and insignificant in the eyes of the world, or in the eyes of people from other religions who have their visible temples and priests and sacrifices, Christians must remember to whom they belong. Though suffering and facing hardships, persecution and insults, Christians must remember that God the Father regards the believer as His own dear possession, treated just as people value and protect their own property.

iv) We must not forget the response Peter is looking for from this holy and royal priesthood. He expects to see us offering spiritual sacrifices by joyfully declaring God's praises for the gospel of our Lord Jesus Christ, which has granted us new life and set us on this pilgrim trail to an eternal and glorious inheritance. Our readiness to respond in joyful acclamation is an indication of how much we genuinely understand and appreciate what God has done for us. Perhaps we need to be reminded of the position of the unbeliever before God (not mine; no mercy; in the dark) in order to appreciate all that God has done for us. Such an authentic response should enrich our times of gathering together as we declare the praises of the God and Father of our Lord Jesus Christ.

v) So often our lives are focused on work, money, hobbies, holidays etc. All of these may be good things in themselves created by God. Yet they can become idols if we begin to live for them. Peter wants to correct our thinking by making the great purpose of our existence the climax of his teaching here. We have been chosen and saved for a purpose: to live for God and delight in His goodness.

Proclaiming the message
A preaching outline
Title: **'God's People Have Been Chosen For A Glorious Purpose'**
Text: **1 Peter 2:4-10**
(1) A new temple (4-8)
(2) A new identity (5, 9)
(3) A new purpose (5, 9, 10)

Other preaching possibililities
The above exposition has sought to be sensitive to the way in which verses 6-10 repeat and develop verses 4 and 5, but other ways of handling the text are obviously possible, for example:

(1) The platform of the church (4-8) – building on Christ
(2) The privileges of the church (9, 10) – God's chosen people
(3) The purpose of the church (5, 9) – offering spiritual sacrifices

Within 1:22-2:10 Peter has specifically drawn attention to how Christians should consider their corporate identity. Various images and terms are used which, together, form a helpful outline of how he viewed the church. This could be developed as follows:

The church is:

(1) The family of God 1:22–2:3 (brothers, babies etc)
(2) The temple of God 2:4-8
(3) The people of God 2:9, 10

Leading a Bible study

Title: **'God's People Have Been Chosen For A Glorious Purpose'**

Text: **1 Peter 2:4-10**

(1) Introduce the issues

All sorts of labels fly around in our society. We label people who are in some way different from us, often unfairly and unkindly. Are we guilty of using labels like this of others? What sort of labels do non-Christians use when referring to Christians or the church?

(2) Study the passage

   i)   Using Bible cross-references, look up the background and context of the various Old Testament references in this passage.

   ii)   Why is Jesus described as the 'living stone' and what function does this stone have (vv. 4, 6)?

   iii)   What sort of building is God constructing and what is its function (vv. 4-6)?

iv) What are the different reactions which people have to this stone and what are the results which follow? (vv. 6-8)?

v) What is the significance of the different titles given to God's people in verses 5, 9?

vi) What should flow from an appreciation of all that God has done for us in the gospel (vv. 5, 9, 10)?

(3) *Think it through*

i) What was the purpose of the temple in the Old Testament and how is that fulfilled in the New Testament in Jesus (vv. 4-6)?

ii) How do we know from this passage that God is completely in control of His plans (vv. 4-8)?

iii) What is the significance of every Christian being part of the holy/royal priesthood (vv. 5, 9)?

iv) Does 'declaring God's praises' primarily refer to evangelism, or to the act of singing when God's people gather together, or does it have a wider meaning (vv. 9, 10)?

(4) *Live it out*

i) How should the labels that God uses to describe His people be a source of encouragement to you?

ii) How can you encourage each other to declare God's praises in your lives?

8

'A STRATEGY FOR LIVING AS GOD'S PEOPLE IN THE WORLD'

(1 PETER 2:11-12)

Having examined the Christian's relationship with God in order to highlight both future glory and present privileges (1:3–2:10), Peter now turns his attention to how the Christian is to relate to Gentiles or 'pagans' (2:12; 4:3). A general strategy is outlined (2:11-12) which is then applied in society (2:13-17), in the workplace (2:18-25), in the home (3:1-7) and in the church (3:8-12). The specific issue of how to cope when this strategy leads to conflict with the world is then picked up (3:13–4:6), before Peter ends the section by again turning to behaviour within the church as the backdrop for Christians to engage effectively within a hostile world (4:7-11).

The opening words of this section in 2:11 ('sojourners and exiles' ESV) connect with 1:1 and serve as a reminder that Peter views God's people as still in exile. All the glorious privileges of being God's chosen people are to be worked out in an ungodly and sometimes hostile environment. Yet their calling is to live in a way which honours Christ and makes a difference within the world around them.

Listening to the text

(1) *Preliminary observations*

i) Peter's choice of words highlights that this passage is pivotal within the epistle. Firstly, the opening 'Dear friends/ Beloved' clearly indicates a division within the letter, as at 4:12. Secondly, he picks up the theme of his readers as exiles as in 1:1.

ii) Peter has already hinted that 'conduct' (ESV) or behaviour (2:12) is important by its three-fold use at 1:15-18. However, in section 2 it is used four times (2:12; 3:1, 2, 16) and the theme of living amongst non-Christians is uppermost in Peter's mind. The conduct that he has in mind is clearly spelt out here and consists in rejecting evil and doing good. '(Doing) evil' occurs at 2:12, 14(ESV), 16; 3:9, 10, 11, 12, 17, while '(doing) good' occurs even more frequently ('doing good' at 2:14(ESV), 15, 20; 3:6(ESV), 11, 17 and 'good' at 2:12 (twice), 18; 3:10, 13, 16, 21). Of course, word counts need to be carefully handled and in fact Peter uses two different words for 'good'. However, turning from evil and seeking to do good goes to the heart of how Peter thinks his readers should live out their lives as God's chosen people in exile.

iii) Our headline text (2:11-12) also reveals something of the situation of the believers. In Section 2 Peter envisages suffering but in almost every case it refers primarily to hostile verbal attacks (e.g 2:12, 15, 23; 3:9; 4:4).

iv) Verses 11 and 12 adopt a clear structure which will be seen repeatedly in this section. First there is a call to abstain from sin (11), then a call to good conduct amongst non-Christians with the aim of seeing a particular result (12).

(2) Exposition

Introduction: How do exiles live?

Having now concluded section 1 (1:3–2:10), explaining what it really means to be God's chosen people, Peter now returns to his starting point (1:1-2). His aim within Section 2 (2:11–4:11) is to show how God's chosen people are to live out their lives as exiles within a potentially hostile situation. From 1:1 he picks up 'exile' or 'stranger' – which makes it clear that Christians live a long way from home as understood in the light of their inheritance (1:4) – and 'sojourner' (ESV) or 'alien' which highlights the deprivation of certain rights relating to citizenship. The two phrases together highlight the fact that God's chosen people on their journey to God's inheritance never quite belong within this world. Since that is the case should they withdraw from the world or immerse themselves in the culture and show that they do belong by accommodating to its values? Peter advocates an entirely different strategy.

i) You must turn from sin (2:11)

There is a war on within our soul. The 'sinful desires' which used to govern our lives (1:14; 4:2 for the same word in Greek) are fighting within us in order to overthrow the lordship of Christ and are seeking to draw us back either to former behaviour or to the behaviour which saturates the culture. Christians are encouraged to abstain from or renounce such desires. It is a battle won in the mind and achieved in the hand to hand guerrilla warfare of fighting sin in everyday life.

ii) You must adopt good conduct (2:12a)

Verse 11, however, is only part of the strategy. As non-Christians speak against Christians, believers are to conduct themselves in such a way that their good behaviour is evident. Peter presumes hostile verbal attacks all the way through this section, including, as here, accusations that the behaviour of Christians is evil (cf. perhaps 2:15). Peter expects such occurrences as commonplace, and Christians today will recognise the realism of his teaching as they cope with the jibes and taunts which come their way because of their faith in Jesus Christ.

His strategy for dealing with it echoes Jesus' teaching in Matthew 5:16 with the common themes of 'seeing', 'good deeds' and 'glorifying' God. In both instances Christians are to be known for their good behaviour and specifically for their good deeds which will be seen and observed (cf. 3:2). This important theme will dominate much of his treatment up to 4:11. Christians are to be known within the world not just for what they are against (as they battle with sin), but also for what they are for, and so gain a reputation within the world for good deeds.

Peter's strategy (turn from sin and do good) amounts to no more than daily repentance. Each day the believer is to turn from sin towards following Christ and leading a good life which glorifies God.

iii) What are the results (2:12b)?

The purpose behind their good behaviour is that non-Christians who see it will glorify God. It is possible that the act of glorifying God could be the grudging recognition of God's glory by those still implacably opposed to Him, but it is far more likely that it refers to the willing and glad recognition of God's glory by those who now do belong to Him. Such activity will take place on the day of visitation. It may be that this is a reference to the time when the gospel is preached and the Spirit visits in order to work within to grant new birth. It is more likely to refer to the day when

Jesus Christ is revealed, the inheritance is received and God's glory is more fully seen. Interestingly, Jeremiah 29:10 speaks of the day when the exile of God's people is ended as the day when he visits(ESV). Moreover, Jeremiah 29:5-14 provides a helpful Old Testament parallel of instructions and guidance concerning how exiles are to live in Babylon, e.g. 'seek the welfare of the city where I have sent you into exile' (29:7 ESV.)

If this is the case, Peter is envisaging a situation where many non-Christians will have been converted by the time God visits. Their conversion will owe much to the impact of Christians on society around them. In chapter 6 of *Promoting the Gospel*, John Dickson shows how this did happen in the early church. Though such a strategy does not replace proclaiming the gospel, Dickson is surely correct in stating that such behaviour is incredibly important in promoting the gospel. Though we might feel that the most effective evangelism is dependent upon obtaining the best evangelist to preach, in practice the sustained witness of a godly life shining like a beacon in the darkness is incredibly powerful and can sometimes by itself be the means of drawing people into God's Kingdom (cf. 3:1). Of course, we should be aware that such results are not guaranteed. Peter certainly envisages situations where the results are different (e.g. 3:16 where those hostile to Christians are covered in shame).

If 'the day of visitation' is at the end, then once again Peter is seeking to help Christians to see everything in the light of the day when Jesus Christ is revealed. Our understanding, not only of who we are and what salvation is, but also of how we act in the world must be viewed from that perspective. The final day is Peter's unchanging reference point which informs all his teaching.

(3) *Summary*

Peter has a straightforward strategy for how Christians are to live in exile as they cope with all the pressures of living amongst non-Christians. In order to have a beneficial effect and even draw people into God's Kingdom they must turn from sin and seek to do what is good within society, trusting that this will have eternal results when Jesus Christ is revealed.

From text to teaching

(1) *Get the message clear*

Big idea (theme)

Christians are to have a significant impact on the world through the quality of their lives.

Big questions (aim)

Preaching or teaching on this passage should answer the following questions:

+ What is the best strategy for making an impact on society?
+ How is it best for Christians to deal with opposition to their faith?
+ What results should follow from Christians living good lives?

(2) *Engage the Hearer*

Point of contact

A new pair of football boots are bought. As they are taken out of the box they are clean, shining and in perfect shape. However, they must not remain like that if they are going to fulfil the purpose for which they are bought. They are meant to be plunged into the mud of the football pitch where they can do their job. In similar fashion, Christians who have such wonderful present and future privileges (1:3–2:10), must get involved in the muddy world where God has placed them.

Dominant picture
An ambassador abroad lives and works in a foreign context, but will always recognise the need to show faithful allegiance to his sovereign. Similarly, the believer living and working in a 'foreign' country, seeks to live a distinctive life, out of allegiance to his Lord.

(3) Application
i) Peter is clearly passionate about earthing his theology; he is not interested in a piety which is disconnected from the world. Though distinct from the surrounding non-Christian culture (they remain exiles), his vision is that they are to plunge themselves into society (though not into sin 4:4) such that their lives make a difference to the world around them.

ii) Sinful desires constantly wage war against us, enticing us away from God's will. We need to recognise that we are in a daily battle and be encouraged to find appropriate strategies in order to avoid regular defeat. So often we drift with the flow of society, adopting its values and behavioural norms and expectations. These are to be challenged and resisted where they are simply expressions of sinful desires.

iii) We should not expect to avoid some degree of opposition or even persecution and suffering if we follow Christ. Instead, when this happens, we are to respond by living lives marked by good deeds. We are to pursue this strategy not only for its own sake, but also for God's glory, because of its evangelistic potential in causing people to consider why our lives are different. Perhaps the danger for many of us is that we have several compartments to our lives. Amongst our Christian friends we have particular standards, but in the world of work or sport we adapt to our surrounding environment. Peter's challenge is that there should be a consistency in our lives which results in non-Christians observing our good behaviour and being provoked or challenged to think about what it might signify.

iv) Often we do not see the results of our work for Christ, especially in evangelism where words are sown but we do not necessarily see the harvest. We should, however, take encouragement from this passage that God is well able to use our good deeds. The contrast between Gentiles speaking against Christians now and glorifying God at the end highlights the important role of the behaviour of Christians, which stands in between these two events. Under God, such behaviour can be the vital link in the chain which enables critical friends and work colleagues to come to a point where they too give glory to God.

v) Many Christians feel inadequate when it comes to evangelism. Excuses come readily to hand because often our only model for evangelism is the gifted full-time evangelist speaking to a packed crowd. We feel that we are simply not gifted in the same way, and it becomes perceived as an arena for the specialist. However, Peter's strategy opens up involvement in evangelism to every Christian. Peter's strategy enables every Christian to find a role in advancing the gospel through their lifestyle.

Proclaiming the message
A preaching outline

Title: 'A Strategy For Living As God's People In The World'
Text: 1 Peter 2:11-12

Introduction: how do exiles live?
(1) You must turn from sin (2:11)
(2) You must adopt good conduct (2:12a)
(3) What are the results? (2:12b)

Other preaching possibilities
If you do not have sufficient time for a separate sermon on 2:11-12, the material could be incorporated with 2:13-17 or 2:13-25 in order to show how the strategy outlined in 2:11-12 is applied in the particular situations Peter considers later in the same chapter. An example of linking with 2:13-17 would be the following:

(1) General strategy 2:11-12
   i)   How does the strategy work?
       a) Resist sin (2:11)
       b) Do good (2:12)
   ii) What are the results (2:12b)?
   iii) Are there holes in this strategy (i.e. can living a good life really have an evangelistic effect – see 3:1)?

(2) Specific strategy for living under state authority 2:13-17
   i)   How does the strategy work?
       a) Resist sin (2:16)
       b) Do good (2:13, 15, 16)
   ii) What are the results (2:15)?

iii) Are there holes in the strategy (2:17)? (i.e. what happens when the officials are hostile to Christians?)

Leading a Bible study

Title: 'A Strategy For Living As God's People In The World'
Text: **1 Peter 2:11-12**

(1) Introduce the issues

Christians are meant to stand out within society as lights in the darkness. What are the things which cause our lives to be indistinct from the prevailing culture?

(2) Study the passage

  i)   What contrast do you notice between the way God's people are described in 2:9-10 and in 2:11-12?

  ii) In what sort of activities is the Christian to be involved in verse 11? ... and in verse 12?

  iii) How should the Christian face hostility from non-Christians (see v. 12)?

  iv) What expectation does Peter have if believers follow this strategy (see v. 12)?

(3) Think it through

  i)   What do you find most helpful in enabling you to abstain from sinful desires (see v. 11)?

  ii) In what areas are Christians accused of doing wrong within our society (see v. 12)?

  iii) Discuss how Christians individually and corporately could be more involved in 'good deeds' within our society (see v. 12).

  iv) How significant was the quality of life of a Christian friend or acquaintance to your own conversion (see v. 12)?

(4) Live it out

i) How would this passage help to make a difference to your own Christian lifestyle?

ii) How can we encourage each other to adopt Peter's strategy in the workplace throughout the week?

9

'Living As God's People For The World'

(1 Peter 2:13-17)

The Christian communities to whom Peter was writing formed a tiny minority within a pagan empire. A key issue amongst these embattled believers, therefore, concerned how they should relate to non-Christian figures of authority. Should they withdraw from all contact with the state or accommodate themselves to the directives and laws of the empire? Peter builds on his alternative strategy outlined in the previous verses (2:11, 12) and applies it specifically to a marginalised group of Christians living within the Roman empire. He will later deal with how Christians are to live distinctively both in the workplace (2:18-25) and in the home (3:1-7), but begins by considering the fundamental relationship with the state's rulers. In this passage we find a willingness to engage and work with the state, but also clear limits and occasions when the Christian must disobey.

Listening to the text

(1) Preliminary observations

i) Peter will consider three particular sets of relationships which are linked by the common theme of submission (2:13, 18; 3:1). Touching on just one of the corresponding responsibilities in Ephesians 5:22–6:9 (husbands – see 3:7), Peter's focus is especially on the Christian in a vulnerable and difficult position.

ii) 'Evil' (2:14 (ESV), 16) and 'do good' (2:14 (ESV), 15) both occur twice as Peter begins to apply the general strategy of 2:11, 12.

iii) Fear of God is to be a regular feature within section 2 (2:17; 3:2), as was referred to at 1:17. Note English translations use 'respect' or 'reverence'.

(2) Exposition

i) A simple strategy for Christians in the world

A good case can be made for starting the exposition with the command to submit in verse 13. However, for the sake of identifying and reinforcing Peter's general strategy, his previous teaching in verses 11, 12 will be used as the basic framework.

a) Christians must resist sin (2:14, 16)

The state officials and institutions are put there by God to punish those who do evil and to praise those who do good (14). Submission to the state and its laws is one of the means by which Christians are helped to fight against sin within their own lives. Even an ungodly state can enact wise laws which are designed to restrain evil behaviour and Christians will wish to recognise that, for the Lord's sake, it would be wise for them to conform to the law, as a means of fighting against sin. For example, submitting to the modern drink/drive regulations is a means by which all, including Christians, can avoid falling into sin.

Peter, however, goes further than this. Christians must recognise that they are primarily slaves to God and are required to serve Him. Therefore, even if the state permits certain evil activities, the Christian is not to use their legality to cover up the fact that they are evil and products of sinful desires. For example, gambling, property speculation, extravagant purchases and litigious behaviour all fall within U.K. law, but 'freedom' to be involved in such activities cannot disguise the fact that they may stem from evil desires. The freedom of the Christian within the state is a freedom to live as God's slave, doing what He would want and abstaining from things with which He would not be pleased.

b) Christians must do good (2:13-15)

Peter is not interested in Christians simply turning from sinful behaviour. He is passionately concerned that the good deeds of Christians shine throughout society and show that a good life will generally be one where the Christian submits to state authorities.

Rather than encouraging withdrawal from society or protest against its non-Christian rulers, Peter's instruction is that there should be submission to the human institutions of the state. This would mean the basic requirement of doing what each citizen was required to do, such as obeying the laws and paying taxes. Peter himself would have witnessed Jesus' own basic attitude to the state with his willingness to pay tax (see Matt. 17:24-27; 22:15-22). Such submission is to be offered whether to local governors or to the emperor himself.

Part of the reason for submission to the state is that when it is working as it should, its agenda is actually in tune with God's purposes. As verse 14 reveals, the aim of the state is to punish those who do evil and to praise or commend those who do good. In verse 14 Peter reaches a similar conclusion to Paul (Rom. 13:1-7) that the state official is God's servant or minister.

In addition to this theme of submission, Peter now turns to his favourite term in this section – 'doing good' (v.15). The Christian life will be marked not just by conformity to the law, but by a positive desire to do good, which will include actions and activities well beyond what the state might reasonably expect. To do God's will (15) and to live as God's servant (16) will simply involve living a good life (12, 15). Here is the encouragement, eagerly picked up within the early church, for Christians to be known within society for their love, care, humanity and compassion.

ii) What are the results of this strategy? (2:15)

When Christians are involved in society in this way, it will lead to results. This time the result is that the ignorant talk of foolish people (see 1:14 for the background) will be silenced. As at 2:12 this may refer to what will happen on the day when God visits at the end, and experience attests that Christian behaviour does not immediately silence all opposition. If this is correct, then it points to the fact that God's judgment is fair, since the non-Christians pictured here have the opportunity to see Christian behaviour and discover the Christian faith. However, the phrase may have a temporal meaning, pointing to situations where allegations, for example about the lack of love of Christians, are silenced by the presence of caring Christian voluntary activity at the social margins of society. Either way, Peter is clear that the

Christians' method of influencing society is through their good deeds. Where long explanations don't seem to work and where power is held by others, Christians can still make their presence felt through their good deeds. Though such behaviour does not lead to people being converted to follow Jesus Christ, nevertheless it is often used by God to prepare people for receiving the Christian message. By itself verse 15 envisages only the silencing of hostile voices, but this could lead to softening of hearts and in turn the embracing of the gospel referred to earlier in 2:12.

iii) Are there holes in this strategy (2:17)?
Peter could have finished this passage at 2:16, especially as some of the details in verse 17 can be inferred from 2:13, 14. However, Peter has an important statement to add without which it might well be said that his view of the state is far too optimistic. What about situations where the government does not punish evildoers and commend good deeds, but where Christians are punished and evil is rewarded? Are there holes in his strategy?

Peter, of course, was well aware of the possible hostility of the state to Christians. On being told by teachers of the law that he would not be permitted to preach in the name of Jesus, he replied, 'Judge for yourselves whether it is right in God's sight to obey you rather than God' (Acts 4:19) and 'We must obey God rather than men!' (Acts 5:29).

At first glance verse 17 gives every impression of strengthening the law-abiding theme of this passage. However, within the structure of the verse are subversive seeds. Both 'everyone' and 'the emperor' (ESV) are to be honoured (the NIV obscures this but the word translated 'respect' and 'honour' is the same in each instance). At a time when the Roman Emperor was regarded as divine, for Christians to grant him only the same honour as the local provincial governor was a radical move. This may also be the reason that Peter uses the slightly strange phrase in verse 13 ('authority instituted among men' but literally 'human creature') to remind Christians that even the emperor is only a human creature. So by making the first and last terms in verse 17 equivalent, Peter has cut the emperor down to size – he is only human.

Furthermore, though it is right and proper to give honour to the emperor, this is significantly less than the fear and reverence owed to God. In 1 Peter only God is to be feared (1:17); and others who wield power are not to be feared (3:6, 14). Perhaps in Peter's mind there is a link to Jesus' words in Matthew 10:28. Submission to the authorities is therefore qualified. It is only 'for the Lord's sake' that submission is given in the first place (2:13) and at the point where obedience to the emperor means disobedience to the Lord, the Christian cannot proceed any further. Christians are slaves to God (16) to do His will alone (15) and so within verse 17 are the seeds of principled Christian civil disobedience, out of reverence for God. Christians must continue to follow Peter's agenda, fighting sin and doing good, even if they are in a state which has reversed God's categories of good and evil.

Finally, if the first and second terms of verse 17 are compared, it can be seen that though there should be proper respect for all, nevertheless there is a prior loyalty to Christian brothers and sisters. Though involved within the world, Christians will always want to show loyalty and love to fellow believers; this once again sets Peter's submission to the state within a wider context. Love for the brotherhood is an essential part of being born again into God's family (1:22, 23) and is a consistent theme in 1 Peter (3:8; 4:8).

The result of Peter's teaching is to recognise that, though submission to the state is appropriate, it is a submission which has its limits due to our greater allegiance to God and His people. Within that framework, Peter's strategy outlined in principle at 2:11, 12 is to be worked out so that Christians are known for their different lifestyle and values as they continue to resist sin and actively do good.

(3) Summary

Out of Christians' submission to the state will flow a resistance to sin and an embracing of good deeds. Yet their determination to avoid sin and do good will go much further than a mere keeping of the law, and will often soften opposition and pave the way for an acceptance of the gospel. However, where the state is implacably hostile to God's people, the prior importance of obedience to God rather than men is clear.

From text to teaching

(1) Get the message clear

Big idea (theme)

Christians are to be fully engaged within society and are to be known for their good deeds.

Big questions (aim)

Preaching or teaching on this passage should answer the following questions:

+ How should Christians engage with the state authorities?
+ What can Christians expect to be the result of such engagement?

✦ When is it appropriate not to submit to the state authorities?

(2) *Engage the hearer*
Point of contact
A military leader, a football manager or a chief executive of a manufacturing firm share a common aim to find and implement a strategy which is going to work and make a difference. Likewise Peter wants Christians, though in a minority, to develop a strategy for making an impact on society.

Dominant picture
Peter speaks of the danger of using our freedom as a 'cover-up' for evil. We hear of politicians finding a good day 'to bury bad news' and news being 'spun' to avoid the truth. All these are illustrations of trying to cover things up so that they won't be noticed. The Christian, however, must seek to live in such a way that no cover-ups are required.

(3) *Application*
i) As Christians we are to be fully involved in our society, avoiding pietistic withdrawal. All of life is to be lived under the Lordship of Christ and therefore the state is also to be an arena where Christians are to show godly behaviour – indeed it should be recognised that for Christians to serve within the state is a high calling as, when the state is working as it should (2:14), it is an instrument for serving God's purposes within the world.
ii) We must constantly examine the quality of our Christian living. Are we as local churches known for our good deeds and our involvement in serving others? Are there initiatives we could pursue at a local level which would demonstrate

Christian love and be a means of silencing criticism? Peter's desire, however, is not for mere conformity to the law; that is the minimum standard, not the maximum. His vision is for Christians to go much further as they avoid sinful behaviour which is not consistent with a holy life (1:15-16), even if legitimate in the eyes of the state, and actively promote things that are good.

iii) It might not be straightforward to know at what point we can no longer obey men out of reverence for God, and therefore we need to pray for wisdom and courage in such situations. There will need to be a willingness also to strengthen brothers and sisters elsewhere in the world (5:9), who have had to make a choice between God and ruler (2:17) and suffer accordingly, by standing with them.

Proclaiming the message

A preaching outline

Title: 'Living As God's People For The World'

Text: **1 Peter 2:13-17**

(1) A simple strategy for Christians in the world

   i)   Resist sin

   ii)   Doing good

(2) What are the results of this strategy?

(3) Are there holes in this strategy?

Other preaching possibilities

A full New Testament picture of how Christians should relate to the state will certainly include this passage along with Romans 13:1-7, Revelation 13:1-10 and Mark 12:13-17. 1 Peter 2:13-17 will be a good place to start, given its positive yet realistic teaching and its author's own experiences at the hands of the Jewish and Roman authorities.

If 2:13-17 is handled separately then the preacher will need to be aware of the context set out in 2:11, 12 and the broader context of the sweep of the whole letter set out at 1:1. Looked at by itself, the passage could be preached in a very 'static' way, whereas the wider context of the recognition of suffering (1:6) and the theological importance of what it is for Christians to remain in exile (1:1; 2:11) provide a much more dynamic approach – showing how Christians as exiles are pushing on towards the day when Jesus Christ is revealed.

Leading a Bible study

Title: **'Living As God's People For The World'**
Text: **1 Peter 2:13-17**

(1) Introduce the issues

'Things just seem to be getting worse and worse but there is no point in trying to change things because the church is so small and ineffective.' To what extent do you identify with this statement?

(2) Study the passage

   i)   To whom should we submit (vv. 13, 14)?
   ii)   What is the purpose of the state authorities when they work as they should (v. 14)?
   iii) How should Christians be engaging with the world in verse 15 … and in verse 16?
   iv)   What should be the result of living a godly life according to verse 15?
   v)   How does Peter distinguish the Christian's attitude to the different groupings in verse 17?

(3) *Think it through*

  i)   What should be your attitude to the government at both local and national level (vv. 13, 14)?

  ii) In what sort of ways could Christians be better at making an impact on our society (vv. 15, 16)?

 iii) Are there 'good' things you could do in your own community which might have the effect of silencing opposition to the gospel (v. 15)?

 iv) Are there situations where it might be right to disobey the government and, if so, how should it be done (v. 17)?

(4) *Live it out*

  i)   How will this passage help to get your church family to make more of an impact on the surrounding culture?

  ii) How can we encourage Christians around the world (see 5:9) who, out of reverence for God, often have to disobey their governing authorities?

10

'LIVING AS GOD'S PEOPLE
IN THE WORKPLACE'

(1 PETER 2:18-25)

Peter continues to develop his strategy of how Christians are to make an impact on the world around them. Having set out the general principles of his strategy (2:11, 12) and applied it to relationships with state officials (2:13-17), he now deals with relations within the workplace (which would often be the home of the 'master').

The teaching in this passage is distinctive in its use of Christ's sufferings and the cross within Peter's argument (2:21-25). Though 2:24 is often lifted out of context and used as a message to non-Christians about the work of Christ on the cross, we need to recognise that this passage is directed primarily to Christians. The message of the cross is for both non-Christian and Christian. For some the message of the cross is left behind after they receive forgiveness of sins and new life through it, and though they are grateful for its work it is regarded as irrelevant to their ongoing life as believers. This is a long way from Peter's view of the significance of the cross. If the work of Christ on the cross gets us into the Kingdom and sustains us in it day by day, it is the example of Christ on the cross which directs how we travel and live within God's Kingdom. In that sense we never leave the cross behind but derive from it, as here, clear insights which show us how to live as believers even in the most difficult situations. Peter's simple strategy, outlined at 2:11, 12 and developed from 2:13 onwards is, therefore, ultimately based on living like Christ. It is Christ-centred and cross-shaped. No wonder it can have such evangelistic potential (2:12)!

Listening to the text
(1) Preliminary observations

i) The themes of submission (2:13, 18; 3:1) and 'doing good' (2:14, 15, 20; 3:6) bind this section to the preceding and following passages.

ii) Translations vary in how they handle the word 'respect' in 2:18, which also occurs in similar fashion later (3:2, 15). Translated this way, it implies an attitude in our relationships with other people. However, a good case can be made to suggest that the word should be translated as at 1:17 and 2:17 to mean 'fear' or 'reverence' and has more to do with our relationship with God. This is the view of commentators such as Michaels and Davids. This would fit with the overall direction of Peter's thinking that, though the Christian is to respect everyone, the only person we are to fear is God Himself. The attitude of submission, whether to rulers, masters or husbands is to be set within the overarching duty to fear God.

iii) This passage develops in an expected manner in verses 18-20 as Peter develops the themes set out originally at 2:11, 12. However, at verse 21 Peter introduces Jesus Christ as an example in a way which makes this passage distinct from the other texts which encourage submission.

(2) Exposition
i) A strategy for the workplace (2:18-20)

As at 2:13 Peter starts with a call for submission which, in the workplace context, is a call to do the job required. As such, it forms the basic plank in workplace relationships both in highlighting sinful behaviour, where jobs have not been done adequately and in revealing good behaviour, where obedience and faithfulness have been exhibited in the completion of tasks.

The call to submission is directed to household servants (ESV). Peter reserves the word slave for the believer's relationship with God (2:16). Submission amounts to the servant doing what is expected of him and applies not only where the master is good and gentle but also where the master is harsh and ungrateful. The term Peter uses of the harsh master is the same used at the end of his Pentecost sermon at Acts 2:40, where it is often translated as 'crooked'.

However, though servants cannot pick and choose which masters they are prepared to obey, their submission is qualified in one important respect. In the same way that fear of God qualifies submission to the state authorities (see 2:17) so such an attitude qualifies submission to masters. As Peter goes on to address situations of unjust suffering, he may well be acknowledging that there will be times when servants have to choose whether to obey God or the master, and they can expect serious repercussions if they decide that, out of reverence to God, they cannot follow their master's instructions.

How should servants respond if they do suffer as a result of principled actions? How are they supposed to act if their boss is harsh? The structure of these two verses helps to outline Peter's response:

A. God's grace/commendation (19a)

   B. Suffering unjustly (19b)

      C. Suffering due to your sin (20a)

   B. Suffering unjustly for doing good (20b)

A. God's grace/commendation (20c)

a) Avoid sin

Starting in the centre, it can be seen that while your master may be inconsiderate and cruel and the punishment may be out of proportion to the offence, there can be no credit for the servant who has wilfully sinned against God. It is an outworking of the general teaching in this section, which is that Christians must abstain from sin (2:11, 16).

b) Do good

Either side of the central point Peter considers the person whose suffering is unjust (19) and results from doing good (20) – a poor reward for their good behaviour. In both verses we are told that the servant endures the suffering. Though a very difficult position to be in, Peter's main concern is that wherever Christians find themselves, including the workplace, they must be seen to be doing good (2:12, 15).

c) Results?

In 2:11, 12 and 2:13-17 results flow from Christians doing good. Sometimes people are converted (2:12); at other times opposition to the Christian faith is silenced (2:15). Here, the faithful Christian can expect God's commendation as a seal of His favour. This appears twice (19a, 20c), as if to confirm it. So even if the boss is not impressed by the good work of the Christians on his staff, God is impressed.

ii) A model for the workplace (2:21-25)

Peter's teaching to servants could have ended at verse 20, but he now reinforces it by introducing the example of a servant who also suffered unjustly - the Lord Jesus Christ – relying heavily on Isaiah 53, which is particularly appropriate with its reference to a suffering servant in an exilic setting.

Christians are called to follow in Jesus' footsteps. If He suffered then we are also to expect a degree of suffering. He is an example, which means that His life is to be an outline for us to trace over and embody in our own lives. Peter has in mind the sufferings Jesus Christ experienced before His death, because it is the way Jesus responded to His suffering which is uppermost in Peter's mind at this point.

So how did Jesus respond to His sufferings? His example is revealed in Isaiah 53 and relayed to us by Peter through the framework he has been using since 2:11.

a) Jesus avoided sin (2:22, 23)

Though like the servant in being treated unjustly (19), Jesus did not commit any sin in the way He responded. Isaiah records that this was the case because no deceit was found in His mouth (22) which is unpacked for us in verse 23. Though suffering, He did not retaliate by returning insults to those who insulted Him even though for us that might have been the most natural reaction. Neither did He threaten His tormentors with God's judgment or call down curses from God. Rather, He entrusted Himself quietly to the God who would bring justice. Jesus, entrusting His situation to God, might include not only the prayer, 'Father, into your hands I commit my spirit' (Luke 23:46), but also, 'Father, forgive them, for they do not know what they are doing' (Luke 23:34). Either way, He avoided a sinful response at a point when He was suffering painfully and unjustly.

This model for how Christians are to respond is referred to again by Peter at 3:9, 'Do not repay evil with evil or insult with insult'. Peter's focus is especially on the verbal response of Christians to non-Christians (see 3:9-12, 15, 16).

b) Jesus died for us on the cross (2:24a)

As Peter has now given an example of Jesus avoiding sin amidst suffering, some commentators see verses 24, 25 as unnecessary to the argument and included only because Peter felt he had to mention something about the cross. However, once we recognise Peter's strategy as a framework for Christian behaviour, we can see that there is a much clearer purpose behind these two verses.

Not only did Jesus avoid a sinful response during His suffering but He also continued in His path of doing God's will by carrying or bearing our sins in His body on the tree. This term for the cross is a favourite of Peter's in his early sermons (see Acts 5:30; 10:39).

As Christians we are called to do good deeds (2:12, 15, 20), yet Jesus Christ voluntarily taking our sins when He died on the cross is the supreme 'good deed' in history. Though without sin Himself, He bore our sins. His suffering and death on the tree was as a substitute for us. Moreover, since death on the tree was reserved for those under God's curse (Deut. 21:22, 23), it shows that a penalty was being paid by Jesus. All the ingredients for the doctrine of penal substitutionary atonement are to be found within these verses.

At this point Jesus ceases to be an example, since Christians, who are the recipients of Jesus' work on the cross, cannot bear the sins of others. Nevertheless, the pattern of Jesus' suffering is still instructive as our 'good deeds' are ultimately to follow the pattern of the cross of Jesus Christ.

iii) Results (2:24bc, 25)

We have already seen the results which flow from Christians doing good (2:12, 15, 19, 20). Now we are given the ultimate example of what happens when Christ does God's will amidst suffering.

First, we were ensnared in our sins, but the result of the cross is that sin's hold has been broken and we are able to live a life of righteousness (24b). Second, we were spiritually sick due to the effect of sin in our life, but the result of Christ's good work is that we are now restored to spiritual health (24c). Third, we were lost having gone astray like a wayward sheep, but as a result of Jesus' death we have now returned to Jesus the Shepherd who watches over us as an Overseer who has the responsibility of caring for our souls (25).

All three results relate to the same experience but view it from different angles. Together they highlight the richness of what Jesus' death on the cross has accomplished and what conversion signifies. It brings new life. It is spiritual healing and restoration. It is returning to the Shepherd to live under His guidance and rule. Notably Peter uses the same word in Acts 3:19 translated turn, as is translated return in 2:25, as he encourages his hearers to turn to God in order to experience forgiveness and refreshment. Likewise on the evening before He died, with Peter present, Jesus said that the shepherd would be struck and the sheep would be scattered (Mark 14:27). Now on the other side of the cross Jesus the Shepherd is gathering His sheep. These are the glorious results which flow from Jesus' determination to avoid any sinful responses whilst suffering and to pursue His given task to the end.

As ever, when Peter speaks of Jesus' suffering and death, he concludes by reminding us that Jesus Christ is alive

– as the Shepherd and Overseer of our souls. Peter is now bringing his teaching full circle. To those who suffer unjustly for doing good in their workplace, Peter has offered Jesus Christ as an example to follow both in their sufferings and in doing good deeds. Yet he has done more than that by going on to remind them not only what Christ's death achieved for them, but also that Christ's current ministry is to watch over and care for each sheep within the flock. At this point the model or example of Jesus Christ gives way to the reality of the present comfort of living under His Shepherd-like care and compassion, for He of all people understands what servants who suffer unjustly are experiencing day by day. Both through past example and present ministry, Jesus Christ is to be the focus of their attention.

Therefore, those servants who are branded with suffering, like Jesus the suffering servant (see Isa. 53), have been branded with the cross, the sign of Christ. It is a sign to Christ that these servants really belong to Him, the loving Shepherd who cares for all His sheep. It is a sign to believers that they are following in Jesus' footsteps (cf. 2:21), no longer going astray (2:25) and assured of Jesus' Shepherd-like care. It is also, however, a sign to a watching world. As suffering Christians embody the cross in the workplace or elsewhere, so they point beyond their own sufferings to the reality of Christ's sufferings and death on the cross and the greatest act of goodness in the whole world. And as unbelievers see the good lives of Christians, might not some turn from cursing God to glorify Him (2:12)?

(3) Summary
The Christian is to make a difference in every part of life including the workplace, however difficult the situation may

be. The simple strategy remains the same. As Christians submit to their boss by doing their work as required, they are to turn from sin and seek to do what is good even though it may involve suffering. They can be confident of God's commendation, looking to Jesus Christ as both a model to follow in His suffering on the cross and as a Shepherd who cares for them.

From text to teaching
(1) Get the message clear
Big idea (theme)
Christians are to be distinctive in the workplace in the way in which they respond to unjust treatment, following the example of Jesus.

Big questions (aim)
Preaching or teaching on this passage should answer the following questions:
+ What sort of distinctive behaviour should be shown by Christians in the workplace?
+ In what ways is Christ to be an example to us in how we respond to suffering?
+ What results flowed from Christ's willingness to suffer unjustly?

(2) Engage the hearer
Point of contact
Rummaging through the attic or the garage you might well come across items which you no longer need. Though they may have served their purpose they are now redundant. Such an attitude must not be used concerning the cross of Christ. Though the work of the cross enabled us to enter God's

Kingdom in the first place, it is by no means redundant for those who are now Christians since it also serves as a model for how to live as Christians amid suffering.

Dominant picture

Nadia Eweida was in the news in 2006. As a British Airways official she was not permitted to wear a small jewellery cross at work. Although the decision of BA was reversed, by far the more important issue for Christians is not whether they are allowed to wear a cross but whether their lives reflect the cross of Christ. This is the distinctive Christian lifestyle which will make a difference in the workplace.

(3) Application

i) Whether these household servants were technically slaves or not we need to acknowledge that in some parts of the world there is an uncomfortable similarity between 'slave labour' today and conditions then. However, for most of us conditions are very different. Yet what Peter gives us are abiding principles to be applied in the workplace, as he uses his most powerful argument, the model of Jesus Christ, to inform the response of believers. Therefore, although it may not be appropriate simply to translate 'slaves' as 'employees' nevertheless in our application of the passage we will want to work hard at seeing how such principles can be applied in our working lives. For example, many employees receiving unfair treatment from an employer cannot simply leave or take legal action because of the possibility of being out of work, perhaps permanently. As a result, though modern employees might have a raft of protective legislation which distinguishes them from first-century 'servants', in practice they might both be in exactly the same boat, trapped and desperately struggling to cope with injustice at work in a godly, Christlike manner.

ii) Having noted that there are limits to submission due to our overriding reverence for God, these limits need to be explored. As God's chosen people we have the responsibility to live in obedience to God rather than adopt the values operating around us (see 1:14-17). Many Christians are frustrated that it is precisely in this area of issues which relate to the workplace that the church fails them most and offers little teaching and encouragement.

iii) Jesus' example needs to be applied into real situations. We recognise that the temptation to respond in a 'tit for tat' way is extremely strong but does the Christian no credit. Some of us may be particularly prone to making sure that we are the ones who have the last word in an argument. How much better to restrain our tongues and instead commit ourselves in our situation to God for His help and guidance.

iv) Especially as we consider the closing verses of the chapter, there is much to excite us regarding the results of Jesus' work on the cross. Often it is possible for us to consider the cross in a fairly monochrome way, seeing its results as simply, for example, forgiveness of sins. A closer examination of such texts as 2:24, 25 helps us to begin to see many more of the glorious truths which flow from the cross. Each image represents a reality in our experience which we need to treasure and meditate on so that we appreciate more and more the wonder of what Christ has achieved. And in focusing on the cross, how good it is in the same passage to have a seamless transition to the resurrection and to remind ourselves that Jesus Christ is the living Shepherd who cares for each member of His flock.

v) As we seek to apply this teaching to our lives, it must not be forgotten that the truths being taught must also be upheld and defended. There will always be those who see the cross as merely an example and deny penal substitutionary atonement. However, this passage reminds us that though it is legitimate to see Jesus Christ's sufferings as an example, the doctrine of penal substitution is tied to Jesus' death on the cross and is vital to any understanding of His achievements. The results of 24, 25 do not flow from Jesus' example, but from His substitutionary death. To deny this doctrine cuts out the heart from this passage and leaves no explanation for the wonderful changes set out at the end. It will always be important to contend graciously for these truths when they are under attack.

Proclaiming the message

A preaching outline

Title: 'Living As God's People In The Workplace'

Text: **1 Peter 2:18-25**

(1) A strategy for the workplace (18-20)

   i)   Avoid sin
   ii) Do good
   iii) Results

(2) A model for the workplace (21-25)

   i)   Jesus avoided sin
   ii) Jesus died for us on the cross
   iii) Results

Other preaching possibilities

Having seen how the same strategy is applied in each part of 2:11-25 it makes preaching this in one section fairly straightforward, perhaps using 2:11, 12 as the framework, illustrating what is meant from the different sub-sections. Peter's strategy for exiles:

(1) Avoid sin (2:11)
- *i)*   In the world (2:16)
- *ii)*   In the workplace (2:20a) (like Jesus 2:21-23)

(2) Do good (2:12a)
- *i)*   In the world (2:15)
- *ii)*   In the workplace (2:19, 20) (compare with Jesus 2:24)

(3) Results (when you adopt this strategy …) (2:12b)
- *i)*   Some are converted (2:12, 24, 25)
- *ii)*   Some are silenced (2:15)
- *iii)*   You are commended (2:19, 20)

Verses 24, 25 provide sufficient material for an evangelistic presentation enabling the preacher to focus on the work of the cross and the difference it makes.

(1) What did Christ do on the cross? (2:24a)
- *i)*   He bore our sins – substitution
- *ii)*   He took our punishment – the curse – penal substitution

(2) What difference does the cross make? (2:24b, 24c, 25)
- *i)*   The dead are made alive
- *ii)*   The sick are healed
- *iii)*   The lost are found

Leading a Bible study

Title: **'Living As God's People In The Workplace'**

Text: **1 Peter 2:18-25**

(1) Introduce the issues

Consider situations where you have seen others being treated unfairly in the workplace. In what sort of ways did they react?

(2) Study the passages

i)   What should be the basic attitude of servants to their masters (vv. 18-20)?

ii)   To what extent should their behaviour change if the master is harsh and inconsiderate (vv. 18-20)?

iii) In this passage what does God particularly commend (vv. 19, 20)?

iv)   In what ways is Christ to be an example to us (vv. 21-23)?

v)   What results flowed from Christ's suffering (vv. 24, 25)?

vi)   How is verse 25 a further encouragement to Christians who are facing unjust suffering?

(3) Think it through

i)   How appropriate is it to apply teaching about first century household servants to twenty-first century employees (vv. 18-20)?

ii)   How should we respond to unjust suffering in the workplace bearing in mind both verses 18-20 and verses 13, 14?

iii) Why does Peter preach the message of the cross to Christians (vv. 21-25)?

iv)   In what different ways could meditating on the cross of Christ each day be helpful to the Christian (vv. 21-25)?

(4) Live it out

i)   How will this passage help Christians to be better equipped to live distinctive godly lives in the workplace?

ii)   How can the cross of Christ become more central to our witness in the workplace through our lifestyle … and through our lips?

11

'LIVING AS GOD'S PEOPLE
IN THE HOME'

(1 PETER 3:1-7)

As believers, all of life is to be lived distinctively under the Lordship of Jesus Christ. It is no surprise therefore to find Peter dealing next with relationships between husbands and wives and in the home, nor that he continues to use his general strategy outlined at 2:11, 12.

Peter characteristically deals with Christians who face difficult situations due to their lack of power to affect what happens within a given relationship. As a minority, the Christians to whom Peter wrote would certainly have lacked power in their dealings with the state. Likewise the Christian servant would have had little power when on the receiving end of ill-treatment from the boss referred to in 2:20. Seen in this light it is not surprising that Peter deals with a very specific situation when it comes to marriage: a Christian wife married to a non-Christian husband. Given the way marriage functioned in the first century we again see a situation where the Christian wife has very little power to alter things by herself.

Peter is therefore earthing his teaching in difficult cases to test out and apply his strategy. And in each case his teaching is profoundly counter-cultural. Whereas in our own society our automatic reaction to difficulty is the exercise of power to assert our rights, Peter encourages Christians in positions of weakness to adopt his strategy of Christ-like, cross-shaped living, trusting that God will work through their weakness to bring about changes which will glorify His name.

Listening to the text

(1) *Preliminary observations*

i) Peter turns again to consider what is of lasting imperishable value. Into his existing list (1:4, 7, 18f, 23) can now be added 'a gentle and quiet spirit' (3:4), which is of great value in God's eyes.

ii) In this passage all of the three ingredients prominent since 2:11-12 are present but in a different order, starting with the result that a Christian woman married to an unbelieving husband would want – the conversion of her husband. Peter's argument is reinforced in verses 5 and 6 by an example drawn from the Old Testament, with parallels between verses 1-2 and 5-6. In both passages there is the encouragement to submit (1, 5) and the reference to fear – fear God (2) but don't fear man (6).

(2) *Exposition*

i) Wives

  a) What result do you long for? (3:1)

As at the opening of this section (2:11, 12), Peter's mind is focused on eternal results flowing from the behaviour of Christians. Peter addresses wives within the Christian family, particularly aware that there would be some whose husbands were not believers. They are described by Peter in his characteristic fashion as those who do not obey the word (see 1:2, 14, 22; 2:8; 4:17). Their deficiency is not so much that they do not have faith but that they are unprepared to obey God's Word – a helpful insight into the heart of the unbelieving husband. Peter is probably thinking of a wife who has been converted subsequent to her marriage and who might find herself in an extremely difficult situation. What should happen if the husband required her to attend worship at a pagan temple? The expectation within society at that time would be that she would follow her husband's lead and she might well find herself having difficulty remaining a follower of Christ herself.

No doubt she would seek to find opportunities to speak to her husband about her faith and hope in Christ, but she may have found that such conversations were counter-productive and fruitless – perhaps even hardening her husband's heart. Clearly her great desire is that her husband would come to follow Christ, returning to the Shepherd, having spent time going astray (2:25). And amazingly Peter encourages her to believe that this can happen without her having to preach at him every day – he can be won over to Christ without words.

b) How can this be achieved?

Yet how could this happen? The answer, linking to Peter's theme set out at 2:11, 12, is that spiritual results can flow from Christian 'conduct', used twice in verses 1-2 (though this is obscured in the NIV). In 2:12 the non-Christians see good behaviour and as a result glorify God. Similarly in 3:1, 2 the non-Christian husband sees godly behaviour and is won over to Christ. The word for 'see' or 'observe' is the same in both cases, highlighting the power and significance of godly behaviour in promoting the gospel, whether within or outside the home. So, what is it that the husband sees that will make him consider obeying God's Word?

c) What to avoid (3:1, 2, 5, 6)

As Peter has already explained at 2:11 she will need to abstain from sinful desires. Perhaps in this particular situation her frustration with her husband's unwillingness to obey Christ could be revealed in an assertion of her views and in not wanting to accept his lead within the marriage. In such a context Peter advises the wife to be submissive (1). She is to do what is expected of her within her role as a wife. This is reinforced by the reference to Sarah as one of the holy women from the Old Testament (5, 6). She demonstrated her submission by obeying her husband Abraham (though the background in Genesis 18 demonstrates her feisty nature). The Christian wife must avoid a selfish assertion of complete independence, which is extremely unlikely to lead to the conversion of her husband.

However, submission to her husband must never lead to compliance with sin and so Peter immediately qualifies his statement in verse 1 with the additional teaching in verse 2. Submissive conduct will also be 'respectful and pure' (esv). Purity may be a particular reference to chastity, but could be a broader reference to the avoidance of sin. Either way we can see that, though Peter is clearly stressing the importance of submission within marriage, he is also carefully guarding such behaviour from being another means by which sin enters the life of the Christian.

With regard to her relationship with God, the wife is to show respect or reverence/awe. Fear of God is to shape and inform Christian conduct as it did in the Old Testament (e.g. Exod. 20:20). The consequence of fearing God is that the Christian wife will not fear anything else (3:6). Perhaps Peter is thinking of a situation where, out of allegiance to God, the wife refuses to be a party to sinful activity within the marriage (e.g. deceitful behaviour, malicious gossip, etc.) In such a situation her principled decision could lead to serious consequences, yet she is told not to fear her husband. As at 2:13 and 2:18 Christian submission to others is always conditioned and defined by the over-riding requirement to fear and revere God. Like the holy women of the Old Testament (5) she should face current difficulties by putting her hope in God with an eye to her future salvation which cannot be taken away.

d) What to wear (3:3, 4)

Though the Christian wife must avoid sinful behaviour through her submission to her husband and reverence for the Lord, this is only part of the picture. She is also to adorn herself in a particular manner (3:3, 4, 5 ESV). Peter uses the same verb three times.

The way to win her husband through 'adornment' is not to be found in the latest hairstyle, expensive jewellery or designer labels (3:3). These are merely external and conform to the standards and values of the world around (cf. 1:14). Instead, the Christian wife is to recognise that real beauty, which is imperishable and lasts for eternity (and is not subject to the ageing process or the seasonal changes of the fashion industry), consists in developing inner qualities within the heart. In contrast to what can be seen (literally, what is cosmetic 3:3), Peter wants these women to cultivate a gentle and quiet spirit (3:4). Though this may appear to be weak and feeble it is neither, since such a gentle spirit is demonstrated by the Lord Jesus

Christ (see Matt. 11:29, 21:5) and is a quality He longs to see in every disciple (Matt. 5:5). Though the world may put a high financial price tag on jewellery, cosmetics and well-tailored clothing, God reserves the highest price tag for the gentle and quiet spirit, such as in Acts 11:18 where it signifies a willingness to lay aside objections and to go along with what God's Word has revealed. A quiet spirit indicates being teachable as opposed to having an argumentative nature. This teaching does not prohibit expensive clothing but it does focus attention on what Peter considers to be the far more valuable character traits of verse 4. Paul deals with similar themes in 1 Timothy 2:9-12.

Though the qualities described in verse 4 are hidden within the heart, they will make their contribution to the visible good conduct which God in His mercy may use to convert the unbelieving husband. He will observe that his wife submits to his leadership within the home (rather than being quarrelsome and argumentative), though at times he will see that she cannot comply with him out of her loyalty to God. He will notice that she is utterly faithful to him and has a reputation for involvement in good works, both within and outside the home. Above all he will see the Christ-like quality of the humble and gentle spirit at work within her, which he may start to value as much as God does. Peter is confident that rather than preaching sermons at home, this is the strategy which God is more likely to use in order to bring her husband to Christ, and so to glorify God on the day of His visitation (2:12; 3:1, 2).

ii) Husbands

  a) How do husbands regard their wives? (3:7)

Though the assumption at verse 1 is that there were Christian wives married to non-Christian husbands, the assumption behind verse 7 is different. Since Peter speaks of the wife as a joint-heir of the gracious gift of life, he may be assuming that most Christian husbands do have Christian wives. The danger is that such husbands would simply adopt the values of the world around them which might mean acting in a dominating and selfish manner – simply thinking of their own needs and taking their wives for granted. In an age where women were regarded as second-class citizens and often as no more than chattels Peter's teaching is revolutionary.

The overriding concern is that the Christian husband is to be considerate of his wife. Literally he is to know how to live with her. Perhaps this is a contrast to the ignorance of the world around (1:14; 2:15). Being considerate will involve a recognition of both the physical and spiritual condition of his wife. He will consider first that his wife is physically different from him, described as the 'weaker partner'. On the whole the wife is likely to be physically weaker than her husband. He must not get his own way through physical intimidation or violence, but is to be considerate and aware of her needs and feelings in order to love her and care for her.

He will also consider his wife's spiritual situation, recognising that, like him, she is an heir of the gracious gift of life. She shares with him the glorious inheritance that awaits every believer on the day the Lord Jesus Christ is revealed, when, through God's amazing generosity, Christians will enjoy life in glory (1:3-12). In that respect she is just as important as he is in God's sight and therefore he should honour her as one who will receive glorious things from God's hand. Even if the world around overlooks his wife (perhaps because she has less education or fewer qualifications or a less prestigious job in that particular cultural setting etc.) he will view her through God's eyes.

Together these two examples reveal both how a husband is to live with his wife in a considerate manner, and the creation pattern that men and women are equal and different.

b) How does God regard husbands? (3:7)

As so often in this part of 1 Peter, when Christians are involved in living godly lives there are spiritual results which flow from their actions. Here we are informed that if the Christian husband fails to be considerate to his wife (perhaps through physical intimidation or selfishness), or if he treats his wife as spiritually inferior, then his prayers will be hindered. God will simply not listen. If husbands are not prepared to regard their wives in the correct way, then God will not be prepared to listen to them. In the next passage (3:8-12) Peter will remind his readers generally that the Lord's ears are open to the prayers of the righteous, but His face is against those who do evil (3:12). Not to be considerate to your wife must therefore be 'evil' since the consequences are the same – God won't listen to your prayers. On the other hand if you do act in a considerate and godly way then the blessings are enormous – God hears your cry ... and will answer as He thinks best. It is an amazing privilege to have God hearing your prayers, and the gateway to this blessing comes through husbands being considerate in the home!

(3) Summary

As Christians seek to do good deeds and embrace a godly lifestyle in marriage, spiritual results flow. In this example Peter has reversed his normal procedure by putting the desired results first. Do you want to see your husband converted? Then adorn yourself with a gentle and quiet spirit, mirroring qualities from Christ's life. As a husband, do you want to see your prayers answered and receive God's blessing? Then start acting in a considerate way to your wife. It's all very practical, challenging and down to earth. Yet glorious results can flow from godly behaviour.

From text to teaching
(1) Get the message clear
Big idea (theme)

Christian wives are to seek the conversion of their husbands through their distinctive godly lifestyle, and Christian husbands are to seek God's blessing through living considerately with their wives.

Big questions (aim)

Preaching or teaching on this passage should answer the following questions:

+ How can people be converted 'without words'?
+ What sort of behaviour should Christian wives avoid?
+ What sort of behaviour should be exhibited by Christian wives?

(2) Engage the hearer
Point of contact

The usual method of getting what we want is through the exercise of power. This may take different forms, depending upon the circumstances. A nation may use military force, a company might use its financial muscle and in family relationships we often resort to persuasive words and arguments. Though this may be the normal way people get things done, Peter wants us to think in a counter-cultural way. The only weapon he wishes the Christian wife to wield is the power of a godly life.

Dominant picture

There is a well-known fable about how the wind and the sun tried to get a coat off a traveller. The wind used all its force but only succeeded in causing the man to button his coat up and wrap it around his body more tightly. The sun on the other hand succeeded in encouraging the man to take off the coat by his own volition due to the warmth of its rays. It's only a fable but it strikes a vein of truth about the most effective practical way of seeing a non-Christian husband converted to obey Christ.

(3) Application

i) It is not uncommon for Christian women to have non-Christian husbands. Sometimes they will, as Christians, have married someone who is not a Christian, but it may be that since their marriage they have turned to Christ. What is striking is how realistic Peter's teaching is. Many in this sort of situation have found by bitter experience that preaching to their husband is simply regarded as 'nagging' and has become counter-productive. Yet at the same time these Christian wives are receiving the message at church that their husbands need to be saved and also that they must make sure that they are sharing their faith. So they follow the teaching of the church but find a brick wall at home and feel the consequent guilt and despair that they are not making any progress. In such situations verses 1, 2 can come as an enormous relief. The Christian wife does not have to preach to her husband at every opportunity.

ii) Teaching about submission in the context of marriage is so out of step with society that it is easily misunderstood. The preacher will often be misheard to mean that he is advocating a domineering attitude by men and that he considers women as inferior. It will be important therefore to balance the teaching on submission with the requirements concerning how husbands are to treat their wives in verse 7. When this is done it can be seen that the picture painted of marriage is not at all demeaning to women.

iii) Specifically, Christians wives need to be aware what it is that God considers to be very valuable in verses 3, 4. In a society saturated with advertising which especially focuses on appearances, it would not be surprising for us to find many drawn to the world's values. We will not resist this trend simply by self-denial or asceticism, but only with the much more positive method of considering what is more valuable in God's eyes. Who is richer, the woman with the expensive clothing and glittering jewellery, or the woman with a gentle and quiet spirit? Another angle on this would be to consider the things which have lasting value in 1 Peter (1:4, 7, 18f; 3:4 and 5:4).

iv) Applying verse 7 to Christian husbands needs to be done in the recognition that many husbands are selfish and their default position is simply to consider their own needs. So often it is the wife who has to consider everything and everybody with the husband taking the line of least resistance and opting out of all responsibilities. There will also, scandalously, be situations where husbands abuse their physical strength within a marriage. In such situations husbands need to be reminded of the call to consider both the physical needs and spiritual status of their wives and especially consider how God considers their prayers in the light of verse 12. Does your behaviour as a Christian husband cause God to turn His face away from you? If that is the case, isn't it time to change and start being more considerate to your wife?

Proclaiming the message

A preaching outline

Title: 'Living As God's People In The Home'

Text: **1 Peter 3:1-7**

(1) Wives (3:1-6)
  i)   What result do you long for (3:1)?
  ii)   How can this be achieved?
  iii) What to avoid (3:1, 2, 5, 6)?
  iv)   What to wear (3:3, 4)?

(2) Husbands (3:7)
  i)   How do husbands regard their wives?
  ii)   How does God regard husbands?

Other preaching possibilities

In the exposition above an attempt has been made to let the flow of 2:11–3:12 shape the structure of the talk. However, there are other ways to look at the text. For example, there is a parallel with the previous passage evidenced by the use of the Old Testament.

2:18-25	3:1-6
(1) Admonition – submit … and fear God (18)	Admonition – submit … and fear God (1, 2)
(2) What pleases God – negative/positive (19, 20)	What pleases God – negative/positive (3, 4)
(3) Old Testament precedent – Jesus (21-25)	Old Testament precedent – Sarah (5, 6)

Leading a Bible study

Title: 'Living As God's People In The Home'
Text: **1 Peter 3:1-7**

(1) Introduce the issues

What would you suggest that most women want in our culture? What is it that a Christian woman with a non-Christian husband is likely to want?

(2) Study the passage

i)   What result is Peter looking for from his instructions to Christian wives (v. 1, 2)?

ii)   What sort of behaviour or characteristics is Peter looking for amongst these women (v. 2, 4)?

iii) What are the differences between the adornments of verses 3 and 4?

iv)   How does the example of Sarah in verses 5, 6 assist Peter's argument?

v)   What two factors about their wives should husbands consider and what effect should this knowledge have in practical terms (v. 7)?

vi)   How might inconsiderate behaviour hinder the husband's prayers (vv. 7, 12)?

(3) Think it through

i)   In what ways does Peter's advice run counter to trends in our society?

ii)   What can help us to see the items in verse 4 as more desirable and valuable than the items in verse 3?

iii) Why is 'a gentle and quiet spirit' so valuable in God's eyes and what do you think it means in practical situations in a marriage (v. 4)?

iv) How does verse 7 highlight that men and women are equal and different?

(4) *Live it out*

i) How can you support, encourage and pray for Christian women with non-Christian husbands?

ii) If you are married, what are the main challenges to your behaviour and attitude from this passage?

12

'LIVING AS GOD'S PEOPLE IN THE CHURCH'

(1 PETER 3:8-12)

This short passage continues to develop Peter's theme as he sets out his vision concerning how Christians should live within the world. From his general strategy (2:11, 12) Peter has looked at relationships within society (2:13-17), the workplace (2:18-25) and the home (3:1-7), and now includes relations within the church family.

Peter returns to this theme at the very end of Section 2 at 4:7-11, while the intervening material (3:13–4:6) addresses how Christians should respond when living a good and godly life brings hostility and persecution.

Given the links between 2:11, 12; 3:8-12 and 4:7-11, it seems that, despite its brevity, this passage occupies a key position within the flow of Peter's thought and it is therefore worth some careful study.

Listening to the text

(1) Preliminary observations

i) The reference to 'all of you' and 'love as brothers' in verse 8 suggests that Peter is drawing together some general points which apply particularly to relationships within the church.

ii) This passage has particularly close links with 2:11, 12 in contrasting 'evil' with 'good' and voicing the same strategy (avoid sin/do good/results), though in a slightly different order.

iii) The passage also develops the theme of 'brotherly love', first mentioned at 1:22, 23, referred to in passing at 2:17 and picked up again at 4:7-11.

iv) 3:8-12 is an important transition passage: it links with both the start and the end of the section (2:11, 12; 4:7-11), and it rounds off the previous passages (2:13–3:7) by introducing a new set of relationships (the church), it also sets up the issue of what happens when believers are harmed for doing good (3:11, 13).

v) The Old Testament quotation is from Psalm 34 (vv. 12-16). It is perhaps worth noting that Psalm 34 clearly points towards Jesus Christ, e.g. Psalm 34:20 and the reference to bones not being broken fulfilled in Jesus' death on the cross. Other significant connections with Psalm 34 include tasting the Lord's goodness (2:3 and Ps. 34:8), fearing the Lord (1:17 and Ps. 34:4, 9, 11), and glorifying the Lord for His deliverance from danger (4:13, 5:8 and Ps. 34:3, 10). Nevertheless, Peter unapologetically applies its teaching directly to the believer. Similarly, he uses examples from Isaiah 53 (2:21-25), Sarah (3:5, 6), David (3:10-12) and Noah (3:19, 20) within this central section, applying teaching gleaned from the Old Testament directly to the situation of his readers.

vi) There are close parallels in this passage with Paul's teaching in Romans 12:9-21, which similarly gives instructions to the church concerning how to operate together, especially in the context of opposition and persecution.

(2) *Exposition*
i) *Turning from sin (3:9a, 10, 11a)*

Three instructions regarding 'evil' are given in these verses. First, there is to be no repaying evil for evil (3:9a) – a lesson already seen in the life and suffering of Jesus Christ (2:23), now applied especially within the church family. Second, using the emphasis of Hebrew parallelism, tongues must be kept from evil and lips from speaking deceitfully (3:10). Third, the believer must actively turn away from doing evil (3:11a).

All of these commands unpack the original instruction set out at 2:11 that Christians must abstain from the passions of the flesh. Though it would be entirely natural to respond to an evil action or insult in like manner, the believer will aim to combat such desires (picking up the warfare analogy in 2:11). Obedience to Jesus Christ and His example comes both as the entry point into the Christian life (1:2) and as the continuing characteristic of the believer.

Again Peter is particularly interested in the response of Christians to verbal abuse. Though they are insulted or reviled (9) their tongues are not to respond in the same way (10). This highlights one of the main issues that was faced by the church, where a mature Christian response was required, following Jesus Christ's own example (2:21-23).

(ii) *Doing good (8, 9b, 11)*

Genuine repentance has both a negative and positive dimension, with a turning from sin, but also a corresponding turning towards God and the sort of behaviour which pleases Him. These are interwoven here.

In verse 8, Peter lists the qualities he seeks within the church fellowship. He uses five terms centred on brotherly love (cf. 1:22; 2:17; 5:9), exhibited in acts of sympathy and compassion (the second and fourth terms). Such love will be shaped by a mindset that both values unity and humility (the first and last terms which both have the Greek ending indicating that the mind is involved). Humility will be picked up later in the epistle (see 5:5, 6). The good deeds that the non-Christians will see (2:12) as they look at the church should include an active love evidenced in genuine care and concern (cf. John 13:35).

In responding to verbal abuse, however, whether from within the church fellowship or from outside, believers are not just to refrain from giving as good as they get. Instead they are to bless (9b) which is literally 'to speak well'. This is an aspect of their calling and purpose as a priesthood (2:5, 9), functioning not just Godward but also within the world to be a blessing (echoing Abraham's calling at Genesis 12:2, 3). Moreover in the Old Testament quotation this response of turning away from evil is reinforced by the command to do good (3:11) which, within a hostile setting, involves seeking and pursuing peace.

These verses portray a positive picture of the Christian fellowship functioning as it should, promoting both love and peace, which is where Peter finishes his epistle (see 5:13, 14).

(iii) Results (9b, 12)

Once again Peter shows that there are spiritual results which flow from Christians living as they should. First, they will inherit a blessing, picking up the theme of the Christian's inheritance which will be received when Jesus Christ is revealed (cf. 1:4). This glorious inheritance is probably picked up in the 'good days' (3:10) to which the Psalmist is also looking forward, and has just been mentioned in connection with the believing married couple (3:7).

Yet verse 12 speaks of other, more immediate, consequences. Verse 12b echoes 3:7 where the Lord turns His face away from the inconsiderate husband. In contrast, those who do good and live a righteous life will find that the Lord hears their prayers, with the implication that He will answer their cries as He thinks best. Psalm 34 develops this to show how the Lord hears the cry of the righteous, drawing close to them and delivering them in their need (Ps. 34:17ff).

While highlighting that believers can be assured of God's blessing both now (3:12) and in the future (3:9) as they live out a distinctive lifestyle as God's people within a hostile world, a hint has also been given that the Lord will judge those who do evil. This lays the foundations for Peter's handling of the situation where believers are being harmed because of their Christian profession and lifestyle (see 3:13ff).

(3) *Summary*

Peter's strategy for Christian living is simple and uncomplicated whether the believer is in the workplace, home or church gathering. There is the need to demonstrate genuine repentance in turning from sin and embracing a good life marked by Christ-like compassion and love. Such behaviour promises blessings from God both in the present and the future.

From text to teaching

(1) Get the message clear
Big idea (theme)
Christians are to be known not just for their restraint from evil, but by their active adoption of Christ-like qualities in all their relationships.

Big questions (aim)
Preaching or teaching on this passage should answer the following questions:

+ How should Christians relate to others, especially within the church?
+ What is the sort of lifestyle which God blesses?
+ In what ways should repentance (turning from sin in order to follow Christ) be a daily experience?

(2) Engage the hearer
Point of contact
The chameleon blends in with its surroundings so that its presence can hardly be detected. Peter is aware that Christians can often find it very easy to adopt the values and practices of the world around. The challenge of this passage is to stand out from the prevailing culture by following Christ's example in our speech and actions.

Dominant picture
Retaliation is built into the way we expect the world to work. Whether you are watching a football match or observing an international dispute escalate on the TV news, repaying evil for evil is normal and unsurprising. Yet Peter wants Christians to embark on a markedly different

route, requiring a different mindset, which leads to a very distinctive lifestyle modelled on the Lord Jesus Christ.

(3) *Application*

i) Our natural tendency is to respond in the way we have been treated. It appeals to our sense of fairness and is therefore a very powerful instinct. We need to recognise that engaging with such instincts is entering a battlefield (2:11). The example of Jesus Christ (2:23) and the assistance of the Spirit who set us apart (1:2) are there to help us survive in the battle against sin, but it is no easy fight. Guarding our lips is one of the first signs of seeking to grapple with our sinful nature.

ii) Sadly churches are not always noted for their brotherly love. Helpfully this list in verse 8 reveals what brotherly love should look like in practical terms. It will involve preserving unity, humbly seeking to work together through disagreements rather than arrogantly trampling upon others and causing division. It will involve an understanding of what others are experiencing (sympathy), which leads to a tender care and appreciation of others within the fellowship (compassion). Peter reminds us twice in this letter to 'love one another deeply' (1:22; 4:8) and 3:8 fleshes out the implications of that instruction.

iii) We are often at our weakest in our praying and therefore we need to make use of every encouragement to pray which we find in the Scriptures. We need to remind one another that day by day and hour by hour 'the eyes of the Lord are on the righteous and His ears are attentive to their prayer' (3:12). Christians are not speaking into a void when they pray. Instead, their heavenly Father to whom they call (1:17) is eager to hear from them in order to pour out His blessing both now and in the future (3:9b).

Proclaiming the message

A preaching outline

Title: **'Living as God's People in the Church'**

Text: **1 Peter 3:8-12**

(1) Turning from sin (3:9a, 10, 11a)

(2) Doing good (3:8, 9b, 11)

(3) Results (3:9b, 12)

Other preaching possibilities

Preachers might, from time to time, wish to consider strands that run through Peter's teaching. For example, gathering together all the references to God's call in 1 Peter (cf. 3:9) we find that the Christian is called:

+ By a holy God to holy living (1:15)
+ Out of darkness into light (2:9)
+ To follow the example of Jesus Christ in non-retaliation (2:21)
+ To bless those who persecute them (3:9)
+ To eternal glory (5:10)

In a sense there is only one call from God which the Christian receives – it draws us into a new life (2:9), with new standards (1:15; 2:21; 3:9) and with a glorious future ahead (5:10).

We could also gather together the various results set out from 2:11–3:12 which flow from living out a godly life within the world. When Christians live as they should:

+ Some non-Christians are converted 2:12; 3:1 (through the work of Jesus Christ 2:25).

- Some non-Christians are silenced (2:15) or opposed by God (3:12b).
- Christians are commended (2:19f), have their prayers heard (3:7, 12a) and receive ultimate blessing (3:9) as they respond in a Christlike manner to those around them.

This could be a suitable framework in considering 2:11–3:12 as one sermon or specifically linking with 2:11, 12 in order to give an overview of this part of the epistle. It may be that in covering the whole of the epistle in expository fashion, giving one sermon to 3:8-12 is a luxury time will not afford. If that is the case then three alternatives are possible:

- Preach 3:8-12 with 3:1-7 giving general application to the congregation after having dealt with the specific issue of the responsibilities of husbands and wives.
- Include 3:8-12 in a sermon on 2:11, 12 to give an overview of 2:11–3:12 before returning to teach the three passages which each involve submission (2:13-17; 2:18-25; 3:1-7).
- Preach 3:8-12 as an introduction to a sermon on 3:8-22. This would enable you to bring the congregation up to speed with Peter's strategy which he has been outlining 2:11–3:7. It would then serve to set up the key question at 3:13 (Who is going to harm you if you do live in this sort of way? Well, it could happen and you need to know how to respond). This would be my personal preference as it preserves the flow of the epistle: 3:13 is not a starting point, but a reflection which arises from Christians seeking to live the sort of life described in 3:8-12.

Leading a Bible study

Title: 'Living as God's People in the Church'

Text: **1 Peter 3:8-12**

(1) Introduce the issues

Peter quotes from the Old Testament about the importance of keeping our tongues from evil. When are you most tempted to respond in the wrong way?

(2) Study the passage

  i)   How would you distinguish between the five express-ions used in verse 8?

 ii)   How does Peter want believers to respond to evil? What response should they avoid and what behaviour does he encourage (vv. 9-11)?

iii)   According to Peter, what sort of results should flow from such behaviour (vv. 9, 12)?

iv)   How does the quotation from Psalm 34 summarise the whole section from 2:11-3:12 (vv. 10-12)?

(3) Think it through

  i)   Which of the qualities listed in verse 8 do you or your fellowship need to work on? How could you go about changing in this area?

 ii)   Can you think of ways in which you could respond to evil or insults with blessing (v. 9)?

iii)   In what ways is the quality of our prayer life linked to the quality of our life generally (v. 12)?

(4) Live it out

  i)   How can we encourage each other to adopt a life of daily repentance (turning from sin and following Christ)?

 ii)   What sort of impact on the surrounding community could your church make if Peter's teaching in these verses was implemented?

13

'CONFIDENCE IN CHRIST'S VICTORY'

(1 PETER 3:13-22)

Up to now in this central portion of the letter Peter has been pursuing his strategy, announced at 2:11, 12. Whether before civic leaders or the boss, or in the home or the church, Christians are to be consistent in turning from sin and doing good. Yet though this may often have a positive effect on society, such a response is not guaranteed and from 3:13–4:6 Peter deals with the situation where believers come under severe pressure or even persecution because of their beliefs or behaviour.

In this passage Peter outlines how the believer is to respond in such a hostile situation by giving some practical guidelines (3:13-17), undergirded by his theological understanding of the person and work of Christ (3:18-22). Only once the believer has complete confidence in what has been achieved by Christ through His cross, resurrection and exaltation will the practical instructions ring true. Peter engages with real issues Christians would be facing as a small minority in a hostile culture in such a way that they can have full assurance of the final outcome.

Listening to the text
(1) Preliminary observations
i) There is continuity with the general flow of Peter's thought since 2:11, 12, with the recurring themes of turning away from evil (3:17), continuing to do good (3:17) and exhibiting good conduct (3:16). There is also the encouragement to show reverence to God (3:15) and fear Him rather than fearing others (3:15 NIV or 3:16a ESV), 1:17; 2:17, 18; 3:2, 6.

ii) However, there is also discontinuity and the passage from 3:13 to 4:6 needs to be treated as a parenthesis specifically dealing with the issue raised in 3:13 concerning what happens when Christians are persecuted because of their faith in Christ. Although both 3:17 and 2:20 speak of it being better to suffer for doing good than for doing evil, Peter is dealing with two distinct (though possibly overlapping) situations. In this later passage he is dealing with the more general situation of Christians being discriminated against and persecuted within society. It even hints at the possibility of being brought to trial where Christians would be required to make a defence (3:15), as Peter had been required to do on several occasions in his early ministry (e.g. Acts 4:5-12).

The difference can also be seen in the way that Peter here refers to Jesus Christ. Firstly, He is depicted as the suffering servant, able to encourage those who are suffering (2:21-24). In this passage, He is presented as the victorious Lord overcoming all hostile forces, as an encouragement to Christians under pressure.

iii) There has been much discussion about how to interpret 3:18-22 and space does not permit me to cover all the possible ways to handle the passage. The reference to 'spirits in prison' (v.19) is notoriously difficult to pin down. Any preacher trying to work out how to deal with 3:18-22 obviously needs to consult appropriate commentaries which can give considerable insight and assistance. However, he can often make headway by focusing on the general flow of the argument, and using what is clear to guide the interpretation of what is unclear. In this instance the context of opposition to Christians causes Peter to give assurance of Jesus Christ's victory, which is developed consistently in 3:18-22. Clarity can be achieved by focusing on the Lord Jesus Christ and what happens to Him:

He suffered once for sins (18)	
He was put to death in the body (18)	Crucifixion
He was made alive by the Spirit (18)	Resurrection
He went ... and preached (19)	Victorious journey to ....
He went ... to the right hand of God in heaven (22)	heaven

The repetition of 'He went' in verses 19 and 22 in the Greek text provides a strong impression that this describes a journey Jesus Christ made following His resurrection. 'Made alive by the Spirit' seems a perfectly reasonable phrase to describe the resurrection of Jesus Christ, contrasting with being 'put to death in the body'. There is no specific reference either to Jesus Christ descending or going to hell. What happens in verse 19 follows His resurrection at the end of verse 18, so in both verses 19 and 22 Jesus Christ's triumph over evil forces is being demonstrated: in verse 19 this is announced and in verse 22 (in words echoed by Paul e.g. Ephesians 1:21-23) His current position is revealed with all evil powers submitting to His divine authority and rule. Verse 22, which is clear, is able to help us interpret verse 19 which might otherwise be unclear. This fits Peter's argument since his readers are facing hostile evil forces possibly making them stand on trial (3:15). Peter wants to give assurance that Jesus Christ has triumphed over all evil and therefore, although Christians may undergo trials, they need not ultimately be afraid.

iv) Regarding the 'spirits in prison', although slightly different terms are used, both 2 Peter 2:4 and Jude 6 speak of angels being kept in darkness or in chains awaiting the final judgment – which certainly has similarities to spirits being kept in a prison. In 2 Peter this is followed by a reference to Noah as in 1 Peter, though in 1 Peter 3:20, 21 the focus is not on Noah's preaching but on the water which saved them, which corresponds to the role baptism plays. Further, it is unusual to refer to people as 'spirits' without any qualification. Therefore, without moving outside the Scriptures to consult other writings, it is perfectly possible to hold to a view which sees those referred to in verse 19 not as people but as fallen angels or 'sons of God' as described in Genesis 6.

v) Baptism can be a contentious issue and teaching about it needs to be handled sensitively. Whereas Paul links baptism to union with Christ and especially to burial with Christ in His death (Rom. 6:4), Peter links it with Christ's resurrection (3:21). For Peter, baptism is the human response of appealing to God in good conscience for a new life on the basis of Christ's resurrection. We need to set this within Peter's theology of conversion. From God's perspective, conversion is based on Christ's death for us, which enables our sins to be forgiven, and on the power of Christ's resurrection, which grants new birth. From our perspective we are to respond to God's Word in obedience (1:2) and faith (1:9, 21). Baptism is simply part of that response of faith in which we call on God for deliverance and salvation.

vi) One of the fascinating things in 1 Peter is that it is Christians who need to understand the full implications of the work of Christ on the cross. Both 2:21-25 and 3:18-22 are written to Christians and set out the achievement of the cross and the risen Christ's current ministry. Yet they serve two different purposes: one helps Christians at work to know how to respond to suffering without retaliating; the other helps Christians to have confidence that evil forces will not win, despite appearances to the contrary. Time and again in the New Testament we see this: the gospel not only saves us (and needs to be preached to the non-Christian) but also teaches us how to live as Christians (and therefore needs to be taught to the Christian) e.g. see Titus 2:11-14; 3:3-7. In that sense we never get beyond the gospel of Christ. This is a classic passage where, as we preach Christ, sinners are challenged and believers are encouraged.

(2) *Exposition*
i) *The threat of non-Christian opposition (3:13-17)*
So far Peter has outlined a fairly positive upbeat set of guidelines to show how Christians are to live as exiles within the world. Despite the difficulties Christians might

have in the workplace which could involve suffering, the
general tenor of the teaching is that the Christian is going
to make a wonderful difference in society. Yet although
Peter is convinced of this he recognises that it is not the
full picture. From his own experience recorded in Acts 4, 5
he is fully aware of the reality of hostility, rejection and
persecution which flowed from the healing he performed
(Acts 3). Kind acts and simple, straightforward gospel
preaching do not commend themselves to all. Aware of
this, and that many of his readers might be struggling to
cope with the application of his teaching at 2:12 because
of the suffering which their good deeds were generating,
Peter digresses from his main agenda in order to deal with
the important issue of how Christians are to respond in
times of persecution. He starts by throwing out a rhetorical
question in verse 13, 'Who is going to harm you if you
are eager to do good?' Although the answer may often
be 'no-one', Peter is preparing his readers for the times
when their Christian lifestyle will lead to conflict with the
non-Christian society around them. He gives some basic
instructions concerning how Christians should respond,
but it is probably helpful for the preacher first to paint the
picture described by Peter.

a) What might they do? – the opposition
Peter gives various hints concerning the situations which
they might face. There will be times when a non-Christian
'asks you to give the reason for the hope that you have'. This
could be an informal conversation where a non-Christian
wishes to discover why someone has turned to Christ and is
looking forward to heaven, but the hints within the passage
seem to point to an experience with Christians likely to be

fearful or troubled because of the suffering involved (3:14). Verse 16 speaks of Christians being slandered and reviled. Together these verses either side of verse 15 suggest that the situation described could represent formal trial proceedings against the believer, especially with the instruction 'to make a defence' (ESV). Even if not a formal hearing, these verses indicate a fairly hostile situation where the Christian has been put into a difficult and frightening position.

b) What should you do? – the response (3:14 – 16a)
Having introduced the issue in verse 13 and explored what form this might take, it is now possible to take a verse-by-verse look at this paragraph. Peter's teaching takes the form of a number of directions.

ii) Remember that God has blessed you! (3:14)
It may be that the natural reaction for Christians who are experiencing suffering is to think that it is because God is displeased with them in some way. Such a reaction is countered by Peter's reliance in verse 14 on Jesus' teaching in the Sermon on the Mount (Matt. 5:10, 11 ESV). This was the very situation that Peter's readers were facing (suffering for righteousness' sake) and so they need to be reminded that in God's eyes they are blessed (not ESV 'you will be blessed"). The tension within 1 Peter is that already believers are blessed (3:14; 4:14) and enjoy all the privileges of being God's chosen people (2:9, 10). Yet they also look forward to inheriting a blessing (1:4; 3:9). At this particular point the focus is on their current privilege. Suffering does not cast doubt on the status of the believer. For both Jesus and Peter it has the effect of providing greater assurance that the believer is in possession of these privileges – you are blessed!

iii) Remember to fear Christ! (3:14b, 15a, 16a ESV)

As at 3:6 there is the encouragement not to fear what man can do against the believer (v. 14b). Coupled with this is the reminder to fear God (v. 16a ESV). Both NIV and ESV translate 'fear' as 'respect' and give the impression that such respect is to be shown to those opposing them. However, a recurring theme is that fear is to be shown only to God. As at 2:17, 18; 3:2 it seems better to translate 'respect' as 'reverence' or 'fear'.

The background to this teaching can be found at Isaiah 8:12ff. Peter has already quoted from Isaiah 8:14 at 2:8 concerning Jesus Christ as the stone that causes men to stumble. Not only does Isaiah 8:12 include the quotation, 'do not fear what they fear' used at 3:14, but Isaiah 8:13 continues, 'The LORD Almighty is the one you are to regard as holy, He is the one you are to fear'. Peter echoes this verse at 3:15 both in the instruction to regard Jesus Christ as holy and also the encouragement to revere or fear (the Lord). This reference to Isaiah 8:12, 13 also seems to indicate that verse 15 should be translated as 'in your hearts regard Christ the Lord as holy' as in the ESV. In his use of the Old Testament, Peter is showing that he sees Jesus Christ as the Lord of hosts and that the natural response therefore must be to regard Him as holy. In doing so, Peter is not just making a theological statement that the Christ is part of the Godhead, but also showing that the two basic responses to God, of holiness and reverence (1:15-17), are now to be applied to the Lord Jesus Christ. Peter wants to contrast appropriate fear of the Lord with inappropriate fear of man, just as Jesus taught at Matthew 10:28.

The main point being made is that the response to persecution, however frightening it may be, is to revere Christ as Lord, recognising His Lordship over every creature and power.

iv) Be prepared to answer (3:15)

Having laid these foundations, Peter now encourages Christians who are on trial (either formally or informally) to be prepared to answer those who oppose them. They are to give an account of the hope that is in them, that is to be ready to speak about this glorious salvation (cf. 1:3, 4, 9) which they are one day to receive and experience fully. In contrast to Peter's own dismal experience, when he was unprepared to answer questions whilst Jesus was on trial, which led to his threefold denial, Christians are to be prepared, knowing that questions will be asked about their allegiance to Christ. Though it is their zeal for good works which may have brought them to the attention of those opposed to them (3:13), these good works are to be explained by the glorious inheritance promised to the believer. These verses do not provide a strategy for evangelism in all situations, but are specifically linked to encouraging Christians to know how they should respond in hostile situations. In this way, though individual believers may not feel that they are gifted as evangelists, they are nevertheless able to promote the gospel through their answers.

v) Be prepared to answer gently (3:16a esv)

Though a readiness to respond is important, the manner of the response should also testify to Christ. Peter's word in verse 15 (16a in esv) is translated as 'gentleness'. How-ever, as at 3:4 (gentle spirit), it is probably better to trans-late the word as 'humility', as it is often done in describing Christ's character (see Matt. 11:29; 21:5). In other words, the way to regard Christ the Lord as holy is to be holy as He is, by reflecting His character in all circumstances. In the specific instance of responding to hostile questioning it will involve humility as opposed to arrogance or aggression. Peter does not want the manner of the response to alienate hearers from the message of the gospel. The way we respond, even if we are not able to win the argument, is vital in our witness to Christ.

vi) What will God do? – the assurance (3:16b, 17)

If believers do respond in this manner to their non-Christian opponents, Peter asserts that their interrogators will be put to shame (3:16b). It is possible that this refers to an immediate reaction in that they will feel ashamed of persecuting Christians for their good behaviour in Christ. However the way the passive mood is used suggests that this is an action caused by God and is probably to be linked to the Last Day. Believers will never be put to shame (2:6) but, though proud and confident as they question Christians, those who stumble over Christ (2:7f), and over Christians (3:16) will one day be put to shame by God. It is the opposite result to 2:12. Far better to suffer now for doing good like these Christians, who are in fact blessed by God, (3:14) than to suffer far worse for doing evil such as those who slander Christians (3:17). God is not mocked and though His servants may be ill-treated and reviled, He will have the last word. Peter is realistic – not all will 'see' the good deeds of believers in such a way as to turn and glorify God (2:12). Some will 'see' such good deeds and rail against them but will stand ashamed on the day God visits. God will indeed turn away His face from those who do evil (3:12) ... forever.

So in 3:13-17 Peter has opened up the subject of how Christians should respond to suffering when they are called to account for their beliefs. Given how things would have looked, with Christians mocked and ridiculed and their opponents apparently triumphant, how can Peter be sure that one day the persecuting unbelievers will stand ashamed? The answer lies in turning to consider Christ (3:18-22).

vii) The basis of Christian confidence (3:18-22)

This section must be considered in its context in order to be properly understood. Though it is entirely possible to use verse 18 in an evangelistic setting because of its clarity about Christ's one sacrifice for sin and the purpose of His suffering (namely, to bring us to God), nevertheless our primary purpose as expositors should be to see how verse 18 (and indeed each of the subsequent verses) contributes to Peter's overall argument as he interweaves two important themes.

a) The victory of Christ (3:18, 19, 22)

Christ's victory over every evil power is the dominant thought, beginning and ending the paragraph. He suffered unjustly for doing good, just like Peter's readers. Though His suffering led to death it was followed by the resurrection (3:18b) with glories to follow (cf. 1:11, 21). So Peter records for us His subsequent journey. This in itself helps us to see that the announcement in verse 19 cannot relate to the time between Jesus' death and resurrection and makes it highly unlikely that it refers to a time before either, such as the view held by Grudem that verse 19 took place in Noah's day.

Jesus' journey following His resurrection is described in two parts, both introduced by, 'He went' (19, 22 in the Greek text). The first part describes Jesus Christ's proclamation on His journey and the second His destination at the end of His journey.

Verse 19 says that the risen Jesus went to the spirits in prison and preached. These would appear to be the spirits who rebelled against God in Noah's day (see Gen. 6:1-7). They are described as those who did not obey, which is characteristic of all who do not follow God (see 2:8; 3:1(ESV): 4:17). As a result they were put in chains (see 2 Pet. 2:4 (ESV); Jude 6) and are now awaiting the final judgment. What did Christ preach to them? The word Peter uses is not his normal one for preaching the gospel (see 1:12, 25) but the word used to herald the arrival of a king or a victory. As Jesus goes in His resurrection body, He is announcing His triumph over sin, death, evil and Satan.

Yet the journey continues and in verse 22 the destination is given: the crucified and resurrected Jesus Christ has now gone to the right hand of God in heaven. In this position all evil powers and authorities bow in submission to Him as they recognise His Lordship. Verse 22 may be clearer than verse 19 because it is a more familiar theme but they both witness to the same truth. Jesus Christ, though He suffered unjustly, is now in heaven and has triumphed over all His enemies. Though the forces of evil and evildoers may still do their worst on earth as they persecute believers, the Lord Jesus Christ is victorious and one day they also will recognise His Lordship as they bow their heads in shame (3:16).

Christian assurance in times of suffering from evildoers is based solely on Christ's triumph over evil, demonstrated in His death, resurrection, ascension and glorification.

b) The salvation of Christ for believers (3:18, 20, 21)

Though the triumph of Christ over evil starts and ends the passage, the salvation which Christ provides for believers is similarly important. Christ suffered to deal once and for all with our sins by dying as a sin offering in our place (the just for the unjust). As at 2:24 the doctrine of penal substitutionary atonement is clearly outlined, along with the purpose of this sacrifice: to bring us to God. It is tempting to interpret this as a current experience of the believer, but it is probably best to understand this phrase within the wider sweep of Peter's writing. The salvation of the believer is primarily future (see 1:3-12) and will arrive when Jesus Christ is revealed (1:5, 7, 9). In that sense Christians still await the final day of glorification when they are brought to God. At present Christians have been brought to their Shepherd (2:25), the unseen Christ (1:8), who will lead us home to God.

Yet this purpose, though to be fulfilled in the future, will not be thwarted and this can be seen from the example of what happened in Noah's day. Peter deftly links the victory of Christ over evil and the salvation won by Christ for believers, by joining together his proclamation to the spirits of Noah's day with the experience of Noah and his family (20). They were saved whilst others were judged when God's patience ran out. They were in a similar position to Peter's readers. They, as a minority, faced hostile, evil forces and under great pressure waited for a day when God would deliver them. Yet when judgment came with the flood waters, eight were saved in the ark through those same waters. The waters, or strictly speaking the God who sent the waters, provided their salvation and carried them to a new world (a new creation, which is the way Genesis 9:1ff describes their new life).

Similarly, says Peter, you are also saved by going through the waters of baptism which will lead to new life beyond. They do not save by washing away dirt from the body. Rather, undergoing the rite of baptism is a sign that you have appealed to God for deliverance before His judgment comes and is effective if you have done this in good conscience trusting in the resurrected Jesus Christ. By this interpretation verse 21 would, therefore, read as 'baptism ... now saves you ... as an appeal to God from a good conscience' (ESV). He has already gone to God (22) but one day He will bring you to God and baptism is the sign that this will happen to you.

Verses 18-22 show how Christ gives assurance to Christians under pressure for their faith. Through His death, resurrection and ascension He has triumphed over evil including those forces facing Peter's readers, however strong they may seem. Through His death, resurrection and glorification He has also provided salvation for believers. Even now their sins have been dealt with, as they also look forward to their journey's end, when they will be brought through judgment to their inheritance in glory.

(c) Summary

Christians may find that living a godly life leads to hostility and persecution. In such cases their conduct must be shaped by their knowledge of Christ. They are to revere Christ as Lord, responding in a Christ-like manner as they answer enquirers and critics. Even if the persecution is severe they can be confident that Christ has triumphed over all evil and will one day bring them safely to God.

From text to teaching

(1) Get the message clear

Big idea (theme)

Christians facing persecution must know how to respond and can have complete confidence in Christ's victory and their eternal security.

Big question(s) (aim)

Preaching or teaching on this passage should answer the following questions:

+ Should Christians expect that living a godly life will always be welcomed by non-Christians?
+ How should Christians respond when called to account for their beliefs?
+ What assurance is given that the forces of evil will not prevail?
+ How can persecuted Christians be confident that they are eternally secure?

(2) *Engage the hearer*

Point of contact

A magnet both attracts and repels. In the same way a godly Christian lifestyle may be extremely attractive to some non-Christians (e.g. 2:12), but may also lead to hostility and persecution (see 3:14-16). In many parts of the world this is the reality for Christians who stand out from the crowd because of their different beliefs and behaviour.

Dominant picture

Following the English cricket victory over Australia in the 2005 Ashes series there was an open-top bus ride through the streets of London for the victorious team before they eventually arrived at the residence of the Prime Minister. Victory had already been achieved on the pitch with plenty of bruises on their bodies to show for it. The tour on the bus was a journey which gave many people (including any Australians present in London at the time) a public opportunity to recognise the victory that had been achieved, before the players ended up at the seat of political power.

Similarly, Christ's victory, also achieved through suffering, led to a journey in which His victory was publicly proclaimed before He also finally arrived at the seat of all power.

(3) *Application*

i) It is easy for us to respond in the wrong ways to opposition to ourselves and the gospel: aggressively and arrogantly seeking to win the argument and prove the futility of any other views, or timidly refusing to respond, or watering down what we say in order not to give any offence. Peter specifically engages with these dangers. To the aggressive, he enjoins humility so that believers reflect the character of the Lord Jesus Christ. To the timid, he encourages an appropriate reverence for Christ which will drive away fear of men.

ii) Many evangelism courses helpfully train believers to know how to set out the whole gospel message. However it may well be, on the basis of 3:15, that we also need encouragement and training to know how to respond to the enquiries and taunts of non-Christians around us.

iii) Our perspective on what is happening in the world can lead to despair. Peter's perspective is for us to focus on Christ and His achievement and current position. Though we do not see Him (1:8) we know where He is and what He has done…and we know that one day we will see Him and He will bring us to God. If we look at ourselves, we will soon lose heart. For assurance and confidence in a hostile world we must look to Christ. He has triumphed over evil and is in the process of achieving a great salvation for all believers who, after baptism, will follow Christ to glory.

iv) As Peter so often reminds us, the work of the cross is vital and 3:18 provides a great opportunity for a careful explanation of substitutionary atonement, but we must hold this together with the knowledge of Christ as the One reigning in glory, triumphant over all.

Proclaiming the message
A preaching outline
Title: 'Confidence In Christ's Victory'
Text: 1 Peter 3:13-22
(1) The threat of non-Christian opposition (3:13-17)
   i)   What might they do? – the opposition
  ii)   What should you do? – the response
 iii)   What will God do? – the assurance

(2) The basis of Christian confidence (3:18-22)
  i)   The victory of Christ over evil
 ii)   The salvation of Christ for believers

Other preaching possibilities
Preachers may want to divide this study into two sections (3:13-17 and 3:18-22), which would give more time to unravel some of the complexities of verses 19 and 20. The danger, however, is getting bogged down in the different theories and losing the wood for the trees. In the interests of clarity it is probably best to keep our preaching on these verses simple and straightforward. The advantage of doing an exposition which runs from 3:13-22 is that it should force the preacher to address the question: in what way are verses 18-22 an answer to the issues raised in verses 13-17? The exposition will then flow as intended and hopefully result in a more sensitive handling of the material given to us by Peter from a particular setting.

Leading a Bible study

Title: 'Confidence In Christ's Victory'

Text: 1 Peter 3:13-22

(1) Introduce the issues

How do you think you would respond if you were threatened with persecution? In what ways do you think your responses would be likely to be inadequate?

(2) Study the passages

i)   From the passage what sort of opposition were these Christians facing (see vv. 14-16)?

ii) How does Peter help Christians not to be overcome with fear (vv. 14, 15)?

iii) When questioned, in what ways should they respond to their persecutors (vv. 15, 16)?

iv) In the context of what we have seen in 1 Peter 1:3-9, why do you think Peter speaks about 'hope' in verse 15 rather than 'belief' or 'faith'?

v)   What happened to Christ after His death? Where did He go and what did He do (vv. 18, 19)?

vi) Where did Jesus Christ finish His journey and what is the significance of His destination as well as His proclamations en route (vv. 19, 22)?

vii) What did Christ's sufferings achieve for us (v. 18)?

viii) What are the similarities between Noah and a believer who has undergone baptism (v. 20, 21)?

(3) Think it through

i)   What are the ways which can help us to 'set apart Christ as Lord' (v. 15)?

ii) In what ways is it possible to prepare ourselves to be ready to give an answer to those who question us (v. 15)?

iii) In the context of persecution why is it so helpful to hear of Christ's activity after His resurrection in verses 19 and 22?

iv) In the context of suffering why is it so helpful to be given the example of Noah (vv. 20, 21)?

(4) Live it out

i) What are the things we have learnt which will help us to face persecution with greater confidence?

ii) Why is it so vital for Christians to keep reminding themselves of the gospel message outlined in verses 18-22?

14

'CONFIDENCE IN CHRIST'S EXAMPLE'

(I PETER 4:1-6)

Contemporary Christians face challenges to their belief and to their behaviour. If believers can be drawn into sinful behaviour their witness will be compromised. Though the challenge to deny the faith would grab more headlines, the challenge to turn from distinctive Christian behaviour is far more prevalent ... and all the more insidious.

If the answer to the challenge to belief lies in the recognition of the triumph of Christ over all evil (3:18-22) the main answer to the challenge to behaviour lies in recognising the example of Christ in resisting evil. This passage reminds us that the pattern of Jesus' life mentioned at 3:18 (suffering, put to death, raised to life) is to be the pattern of life for His followers, who, in their struggle against sin, will also suffer (4:1) before they die and then receive God's final vindication when He gives them life beyond the grave (4:6).

Listening to the text

(1) Preliminary observations

i) The reference in 4:1 to Christ's suffering links this passage to 3:13, 14 and more particularly to 3:18. Christ's suffering not only brings victory over sin and evil (3:18ff), but also provides the believer with an example of how to live.

ii) Peter is clearly developing his thoughts from his headline text at 2:11, 12 with the military metaphor 'arm yourselves' (4:1), picking up 2:11 where Christians are told 'to abstain from the passions of the flesh, which wage war against your soul' (ESV). Moreover, 4:2 picks up the word 'passions' (ESV), also used at 2:11, and 4:3 includes a reference to 'Gentiles' (ESV), also used at 2:12.

iii) The description of Gentile or pagan life in 4:3 and the surprise expressed in 4:4 suggests that the people to whom Peter is writing are mostly converted from a Gentile rather than a Jewish background. Although there were certainly times in the Old Testament when the Jews were embroiled in sins such as 'detestable idolatry' it is more difficult to apply such behaviour to Jews in the first century.

iv) 4:6 poses some difficulties with the reference to preaching the gospel to the dead. Commentators who wish to see 3:19, 20 as evidence of Jesus Christ preaching to the people of Noah's day often use 4:6 to support their position. However, it is important to look at the immediate context each time and recognise the differences: at 3:19 the spirits are in prison and there is no specific reference to their death; different words are used for what is preached; and in 4:6 we are definitely dealing with people who have heard the gospel message preached to them and have now died. The exposition below will seek to explain how to interpret the passage.

v) Of further help in unravelling this passage is the reference to Christ and the link with 3:18. In 4:1 Christ's suffering is clearly held up as an example. In 3:18 this suffering led to Him being put to death in the body but being made alive in the spirit – the same sort of phrases are used at 4:6 to describe the believer. If the cross of Christ primarily achieved victory and forgiveness (3:18-22), it also supplies the pattern of Christian *experience (4:1, 6).*

vi) Peter's view of Christ is extremely simple and straight-forward. Christ has achieved certain things through the cross and resurrection and is now in heaven. On the basis of what He has achieved we now follow Him. Apart from 5:10, 14, Peter does not use 'in Christ' terminology and therefore develops the idea of Christ's suffering and death in a different way from Paul (e.g. see Rom. 6:3ff).

Recognising that 3:13–4:6 deals with the big issue of how Christians deal with persecution, it is possible to detect several themes running in parallel

3:13-22	4:1-6
A. Context: Gentile opposition (14-16)	A. Context: Gentile opposition (3, 4)
B. The Christian response – revere Christ (13-17)	B. The Christian response – follow Christ (1, 2)
C. Christian assurance (18-22) *i)* evil will be judged (18, 19, 22) *ii)* Christians will be saved (18, 20, 21)	C. Christian assurance (5, 6) *i)* non-Christians will be judged (5) *ii)* Christians will be saved (6)

In both cases, though the Gentile opposition is not mentioned at the start, developing this aspect first helps us to understand why Peter is calling for particular be-haviour.

(2) Exposition

i) Gentile opposition (4:3, 4)

Compared with 3:14-16, the opposition here is more subtle though equally dangerous, with the challenge to turn from Christian behaviour. Peter paints a picture of Gentile society at the time, which also serves as a remarkably accurate description of Western societies in the twenty-first century. Their behaviour is characterised by sensuality and passions (cf. 1:14, 18), which surface in a heady mix of alcohol, sex and pleasure. At first glance 'idolatry' seems to be a strange addition to this list, but in Romans 1:18-32 (which also deals with Gentile behaviour and includes the theme of God's judgment), idolatry includes exchanging the truth about God for a lie and worshipping and serving created things rather than the Creator (Rom. 1:25). For Peter the focus on alcohol, sex and pleasure is all evidence of the same misplaced worship.

He then highlights where the pressure comes from: these Gentiles think it strange that the Christians don't join them in all these activities. The image Peter uses is of people plunging into a pool and calling out for others to join them, perhaps remembering times before the Christians were converted and did join in. The social pressure to conform in such situations may feel almost overwhelming. Furthermore, there is the inward pressure which comes from the war going on in the soul (2:11; 4:1) – part of the Christian does want to join in such activities. Finally added to all this is the verbal abuse heaped on to the Christian for not joining in. The word Peter uses is that the Gentiles 'blaspheme' or 'slander' which could indicate speech directed against God, but more likely consists of abusive words directed against Christians involving blasphemy.

All of this creates an enormous pressure on the believer from a Gentile background to revert to their pre-Christian lifestyle. In 3:14-16 the hostile questioning was designed to cause Christians to deny the faith through their lips. Here, the invitations to join in pagan behaviour focus on denial through their lives.

ii) The Christian response (4:1, 2)

As Christians are to respond to verbal attacks by revering Christ (3:15), they are to respond to invitations to fall in with the surrounding culture by following Christ (4:1).

Christ suffered in the flesh when He died on the cross because He shouldered on to Himself all our sins (3:18). It was a transaction done once for all. He is now 'done with sin'. His sufferings on the cross were evidence that sin had been defeated and indicated His implacable hostility to sin and His desire to overcome it for us.

In the same way Peter sees the suffering of Christians as a sign of their hostility to sin and their desire to be finished with it (4:1). Given the context described in 4:3, 4 Christians could easily avoid suffering by adopting the sinful practices of the surrounding culture. No-one would speak against them or ostracise them if they simply joined in. However, the sufferings which come from a refusal to join in are evidence of a desire to be finished or done with sin (4:1); instead live the rest of life for God and doing His will (4:2). Desiring to be done with sin is not the same as never sinning and so verse 1 should not be pushed to mean that we should expect to be sinless in this life.

Therefore if Christians are to resist the enormous pressure to join in sinful activities, they need to arm themselves by adopting Christ's mindset of being prepared to suffer in the battle against sin. Joining in this painful struggle is part of the proof of following Jesus Christ to glory (1:21; 3:22).

Peter's readers used to be content with sin (4:3). In the same way, a homeowner may be content to live with a garden overrun by weeds and nettles. However, in turning to Christ and resisting sin, arming themselves against it (4:1), they now find themselves suffering (4:4). Similarly, the homeowner suffers the scratches and stings which inevitably accompany his desire to rid his garden of weeds. The experience of such suffering is itself a sign of being 'done with sin', in the sense that the Christian no longer wants it to remain in his life.

2:11, 12 continue to influence Peter. Christians will need to live out their life within a hostile Gentile world by turning from sin as they prepare to suffer like Christ (4:1) and by doing good deeds as they embrace God's will (4:2).

iii) Christian confidence (4:5, 6)

Peter ends this section with the same sort of conclusion as in the previous passage: that sinners will be judged and believers will be saved.

a) Non-Christians will be judged (4:5)

The same people who called Christians to account (3:15) will one day be called to account by God. Both those who persecuted Christians with apparent impunity and subsequently died, and those currently alive, will face God as their judge (cf. 1:17). They will not 'get away with it'. Obviously this judgment is not just for those who have persecuted Christians, but it would certainly have given reassurance to suffering Christians in the midst of their struggles. Though Christians may suffer and non-Christians may heap abuse on them, it is God who will have the last word.

b) Christians will be saved (4:6)

In the final verse in this passage Peter provides assurance for Christians who have seen fellow believers go through suffering and die (perhaps due to persecution). To the world it may seem that these Christians have failed and to Christians themselves there may be an element of uncertainty concerning what will happen in the future. Peter wants them to know that, for those who have died, the reason they had the gospel preached to them was so that their future beyond the grave could be guaranteed. Although they may have been judged by men, they now live in the spirit before God. Human authorities may have had the last word about their physical life, but it is God who has the last word about their spiritual life.

Once again the pattern of Jesus Christ is enormously important, since He suffered and was put to death in the flesh (3:18) in a decision which was a judgment made by the Roman authorities of the day. Yet three days later He was made alive in the spirit (3:18) so that He could live before God, at His right hand (3:22). Similarly, for the believer, suffering (4:1) and death (4:6) are to be followed by resurrection life (4:6).

Peter encourages Christians facing persecution (especially considering the threat of martyrdom) to consider the future beyond the grave. Not only are they to focus on their inheritance and the revealing of Jesus Christ, but also on God's judgment and their resurrection (cf. 3:10-12).

So this passage makes perfect sense in its setting. The pressure put on by Gentiles would have led to a real inner struggle against sin. Yet Christians must keep the example of Christ in view. In terms of His suffering He is a model for how Christians cope with sin. In terms of His resurrection,

He is the pioneer who has gone before us to blaze the trail for us to follow. The victory won through His death and resurrection described earlier (3:18-22) enables His life to be a model both now (as we follow Him in His suffering) and in the future (as we follow Him in His resurrection).

3) Summary

Christians will find that leading a distinctive godly life which is different from the surrounding culture will lead to opposition and persecution. In such cases their conduct must be shaped by the example of Christ. As they seek to resist sin they must be willing to endure suffering, which is a sure sign that the believer is resisting sin and seeking to do God's will. They should do this confident of the future, however difficult the present might be, knowing that God will judge the ungodly but will raise believers to life beyond the grave.

From text to teaching

(1) Get the message clear

Big idea (theme)

Christians are to resist the pressure to return to an ungodly lifestyle by following Christ's example and being confident of God's verdict at the end.

Big questions (aim)

Preaching or teaching on this passage should answer the following questions:

- Why are the pressures on the Christian to return to their previous lifestyle so strong?
- How does Christ's suffering provide a model to help us fight against sin?
- How does God's future verdict help to sustain us now?

(2) *Engage the hearer*
Point of contact

By and large we don't want to be different from the crowd. It's much easier to join in and go with the flow rather than swim against the current. This is precisely the situation which many of us face, with the result that we compromise any distinctive Christian lifestyle. It is exactly this danger that is addressed here.

Dominant picture

A premier league footballer has been with his team for a number of seasons and they have a reputation for their dirty play instigated by their manager. One summer the player is transferred to another team and eventually in the new season the two teams meet. The player is greeted by his old manager with the tempting offer that it could be worth his while not to play as well as he might. The player resists the offer, aware that he has a new manager to please, and the bruises on his legs at the end of the game provide the clearest evidence as to which side he now belongs to and where his allegiance lies. Similarly, for the Christian enticed to return to his old ways, suffering in the battle against sin is the clearest evidence of following the new Master.

(3) *Application*

i) Opposition to Christians may take a number of different forms. Though overt persecution is tremendously serious we should not underestimate the difficulty of standing up to the pressures described in verse 4. Sometimes it might even be easier to cope with direct persecution as envisaged at 3:15, since it is much clearer that your faith is under attack and the battle lines are clearly drawn. In contrast, many believers find the situation described in verse 4 harder to deal with simply because to start with there may not be any hostility at all. But the result of joining in is that we will be sucked back into our old ways. It may be of interest to note that the same root word for debauchery or dissipation is used of the lost son at Luke 15:13 as he moves to the far country! To stand for Christ and to live in a godly way will involve the painful act of swimming against the current of the culture when it would be so easy, and so natural, to turn round and go with the flow. As preachers we will know that this is the position in which many of the flock find themselves.

ii) In the fight to resist the culture, Peter wants us to arm ourselves with one particular weapon: the example of Jesus Christ, who, in His battle against sin, was prepared to embrace suffering. This is the attitude we must also adopt. Though God certainly has in view our ultimate happiness on the day when Jesus Christ is revealed (1:7), His current will for our lives is holiness, which will embrace suffering in the war against sin and the lure of the world. Happiness, in contrast, will constantly want to switch sides and walk with the world rather than with God. Peter would ask which side we are on in this battle: if on Christ's side we must be prepared to suffer, but there is great joy even now in following Jesus Christ(3:14) as well as in the future (see 4:6).

iii) Our normal perspective is dominated by our own lifespan ending with our death. Peter wants us to lengthen this perspective to include events beyond death, whether for the non-Christian (4:5) or the Christian (4:6). It is ultimately God's judgment, not men's, that is the determining factor. No non-Christian will escape this judgment – all are included whether currently alive or dead. Therefore this passage should serve both as a warning to non-Christians but also as an enormous encouragement to Christians struggling to cope with the pressures of the world around them. So, in our thinking, we need to encourage everybody to plan not just for the future in this life, but for the future beyond this life.

Proclaiming the message

A preaching outline

Title: 'Confidence In Christ's Example'

Text: 1 Peter 4:1-6

(1) Gentile opposition (4:3, 4)

(2) The Christian response (4:1, 2)

(3) Christian confidence (4:5, 6)

Other preaching possibilities

For the preacher wanting to move more quickly through the letter, it would be appropriate to treat the passage 3:13–4:6 as one unit. As we have seen there is a similar structure present:

(1) Opposition from non-Christians

  i) why do you believe this (3:15, 16)? (attack on Christian belief)

  ii) why don't you join us (4:3, 4)? (attack on Christian behaviour)

(2) The Christian response

  i) revering Christ (3:14-16)

  ii) following Christ (4:1, 2)

(3) Christian assurance

  i) Christ/God will defeat evil/sinners (3:18, 19, 22/4:5)

  ii) Christ/God will save believers (3:18, 20, 21/4:6)

The drawback is that there is a fair amount of detail in this part of 1 Peter but the advantage is that, especially when there are contentious issues around (e.g. 3:19!), it is possible to keep the big picture in view.

Though this passage is primarily directed towards suffering Christians in order to encourage and provide assurance, it nevertheless has an evangelistic dimension, since there is a focus on the behaviour of non-Christians. The following outline seeks to display what we learn in the passage about the Gentiles in contrast to how God views them.

(1) What's so wrong about sin?
  i) How does the non-Christian view sin? (4:3, 4) (sin is natural)
  ii) How does God view sinners? (4:5) (He will judge)

(2) What happens at death?
  i) How does the non-Christian view death? (4:6a) (death is the end)
  ii) How does God view death? (4:6b) (He will give life to believers)

One prominent theme which theologically undergirds all of 1 Peter is the focus on the person of Jesus Christ. This passage is particularly rich in developing this theme.

(1) Jesus Christ
    (He suffered (3:18; 4:1), He was put to death/died, He was made alive (3:18))

(2) The Christian
    (Embraces suffering (4:1), dies, will be made alive (4:6))

The example and pattern of Jesus Christ should neither be developed at the expense of the work of Christ and His victory won through the cross and resurrection (3:18-22), nor ignored.

Leading a Bible study

Title: **'Confidence In Christ's Example'**

Text: **1 Peter 4:1-6**

(1) Introduce the issues

On what occasions do you particularly feel under pressure to join in with ungodly behaviour?

(2) Study the passage

i)   From the passage what sort of opposition were these Christians facing (vv. 3, 4)?

ii)   Why do you think the pressure to join in was so strong (vv. 3, 4)?

iii)   How is the example of Jesus supposed to be a model for us in these circumstances (vv. 1, 2)?

iv)   Who is verse 5 directed at and what assurance does this provide to believers under pressure?

v)   If the people who are judged by men (e.g. in a court or tribunal) are Christians who have now died (through martyrdom?) what assurance to surviving Christians is provided in verse 6?

vi)   What are the similarities between the experience of Jesus Christ (3:18, 4:1) and the suffering believer (4:6)?

(3) Think it through

i)   In our society are you more likely to come under pressure because of your Christian beliefs or your Christian behaviour (vv. 3, 4)?

ii) In practical terms what could it mean to 'arm your-selves' with the attitude of Christ and what is likely to be the result (vv. 1, 2)?

iii) In what ways does keeping an eternal perspective help us cope with difficulties in the present (vv. 5, 6)?

iv) How is the cross to be both the gateway to the Christian life as well as the pathway in it (3:18; 4:1, 6)?

(4) *Live it out*

i) How does this passage strengthen us when we are faced with the sort of opposition envisaged in verse 4?

ii) How can we encourage each other not to be swept along by the pressures of an ungodly society?

15

'LIVING AS GOD'S PEOPLE IN THE LIGHT OF THE END'

(1 PETER 4:7-11)

At the end of the clear progression of the central section of 1 Peter, the issue which now remains concerns how God's people should act together when they are facing times of great pressure and persecution. It is one thing to know that at the end God will judge justly but, in the meantime, how should the church operate to support each other in such dark days? Amidst all the pressures and suffering, the church should be involved in three key activities in order to sustain one another before God's final judgment: praying, loving and serving.

Listening to the text
(1) Preliminary observations
There is an immediate link with the previous passage. Having referred to God's final judgment (4:5) and also to the fact that the believer will be raised to life like Jesus Christ (4:6), Peter continues by reminding his readers that 'The end of all things is near' (4:7). Once again he keeps believers

focused on the future, not only to cope with opposition and persecution but also to shape their behaviour within the church.

There is also a link between the end of the passage (4:11) and the beginning of the whole section. The overall aim for Christians as they live out their relationships in the world (2:12) and in the church (4:11) is that God be glorified.

The other important passage to consider in relation to this one is 3:8-12. A number of themes reveal this to be a vital link in understanding the flow of the epistle:

a)   Just before Peter deals with the specific issue of how Christians are to deal with opposition and persecution (3:13–4:6) he refers to prayer (3:12), which is picked up again at 4:7.

b)   Peter had introduced the previous passage at 3:8 with a focus on church members' brotherly love (3:8), which is also the theme of this new paragraph (see 4:8, 9)

Peter is therefore resuming the subject of how the church is to function in specific areas of its internal relationships (4:7-11) as they support each other in the context of persecution and hostility.

A natural question to ask is why Peter included the teaching about how to respond to opposition and persecution in the middle of his teaching about church relationships. Aside from 4:7a (which picks up an immediate link with 4:5, 6), 4:7-11 could have followed seamlessly after 3:8-12. The answer may lie in the fact that an effective response to opposition must rely on a corporate church family response. It is precisely in the midst of suffering that Christians need the support of their brothers and sisters within the church family to encourage one another to revere Christ amidst persecution (3:13-17) and in the face of social pressure to conform to sinful activities (4:3, 4). Christians on their own may often find the pressures too great, which may be the reason that Peter has placed 4:7-11 after 3:13 – 4:6.

It is worth remembering that Peter had eye-witness experience of Jesus and His teaching, which fleshes out brief references within a passage like this one. In speaking about the need for self-control in prayer (4:7b) Peter may have remembered his own lack of self-control in Gethsemane, when he failed to stay awake and pray with Jesus (Mark 14:37, 38). In the teaching on the need for love in the context of the end being near (4:7, 8), Peter would surely have recalled the observation by Jesus that 'the love of most will grow cold' (Matt. 24:12). And in the teaching on the need for stewards to act faithfully, Peter would have remembered his own interjection as Jesus told the parable of the master returning from the wedding banquet and Jesus' response describing the actions of a faithful steward (Luke 12:41ff; Matt. 24:45ff).

Though the presence of a doxology (4:11) does not always bring a section to a close (e.g. 1 Tim. 1:17) often it does (e.g. Rom. 11:33-36), and as the next verse begins 'Dear friends' (4:12, cf. 2:11), it seems that 4:11 brings this section to a close.

(2) Exposition
i) Praying (4:7)
Peter has already mentioned the subject of prayer. The inconsiderate husband does not have his prayers heard (3:7), but the Lord's ear is open to the prayer of the righteous (3:12). Both references so far demonstrate that it is not quantity of faith which is important for an effective prayer

life, but the quality of life as a believer. This is developed at 4:7. Though the world around and sin within (and also the devil at 5:8) conspire to deflect and defeat the Christian through stirring up sinful desires (4:3), Christians living in the light of God's future judgment (4:5-7a) need to assess such situations soberly (cf. 1:13, 5:8) and exhibit self-control by not falling back into their pre-Christian behaviour (4:3, 4). Out of their desire to live holy lives pleasing to God, reflecting His character, they will develop a relationship where God hears the cry of His children (3:12).

They will need a prayerful dependence on God as they recognise the difficulty of loving those within the church family who have stumbled into sin (4:8), as they struggle not to grumble about all the inconveniences of the church family meeting in their homes (4:9) and as they seek to serve each other with God's Word and strength amidst human frailty (4:10, 11).

Prayer, therefore, is to be the engine room of the church family, enabling it to function as it should amidst all the pressures which might otherwise cause it to collapse. In shame, Peter might well have remembered his own frailty and folly at Gethsemane. He reminds other Christians that the end is near (4:7a) so they will not fall asleep, but rather understand the importance of the times they live in.

However perhaps the main point of 4:7 can be seen when we place it firmly in its context. When the church is faced with great persecution (3:14f) and great pressure to conform (4:3, 4) it is easy for the believer to despair and give up. In such a situation we are to be 'clear minded' by keeping our eyes fixed firmly on the end – the day when those who persecute Christians will be judged (4:5) and believers (even though martyred) are raised to life before God forever (4:6). By faith in the outcome of the gospel, believers are to see clearly through the current darkness to this glorious end. We are to be encouraged and pray to God confident that His eternal purposes will be worked out.

ii) Loving (4:8, 9)

Given the reminder in Matthew 24:12 that, as the end draws near, it will be easy for love for one another to grow cold, Peter wants to encourage and stimulate love within the church family. He would no doubt have been aware that persecution could lead to the division of the church, resulting, for example, from members judging each other when some fail while others remain faithful. To remedy such a situation they are to love each other earnestly or, as at 1:22, 'at full stretch'. This is to be the basic, consistent attitude for the church family to show consistently to each other (see also 2:17, 3:8, 5:9), exhibited in two different but complementary ways:

(a) Forgiveness (4:8)

Their loving attitude will be prepared to forgive and overlook failings and faults. Perhaps there will be some Christians who have succumbed to the pressure and slipped back into the behaviour described at 4:3. Rather than judging such brothers and sisters for their moral weakness, the church family is to love 'at full stretch', by offering forgiveness and encouraging them to live more consistent lives.

(b) Friendship (4:9)

Love is also to be shown in the exercise of hospitality to one another. It would be easy to misunderstand this injunction, since we may think of hospitality as a social activity, linking up with friends. However, at the time, church gatherings would almost certainly have taken place within the homes

of believers. The exercise of hospitality was therefore
vital in order for the church family to have somewhere to
meet. Furthermore, such hospitality could not be limited
to the invitation of friends, but would need to include a
welcome to all who might wish to gather together. Though
the natural tendency might be to grumble about such an
invasion, especially if it included some who had slipped in
their moral behaviour (4:3, 4), their love for each other is
to stretch sufficiently to welcome others into their home.
In that way they can serve one other and everyone can hear
God's Word (4:10, 11).

The gospel is to motivate their love for one another. As
those forgiven by Christ they are to forgive others. As those
welcomed by Christ they are to welcome each other into
their homes. As Christ was at full stretch dying for sinners
on the cross out of love, so believers are to follow Christ's
example in being at full stretch to love one another.

c) *Serving (4:10, 11)*

Having opened their homes (4:9) so that the church family
can meet, they are to use their gathering as a means of
serving each other.

God in His grace has given a whole variety of gifts to
Christians, which are to be used for the benefit of each other.
Those who have received such gifts are to view themselves
as 'good stewards'(ESV), their role being to use their gifts
in such a way as to benefit the whole household. Peter had
heard the warning from Jesus concerning those who failed to
recognise the importance of discharging their responsibilities
before the master's return (Luke 12:41-48). Consequently,
he encourages church members not to take the easy route
and simply look after their own interests, but to take on the
potentially more arduous role of serving each other.

Whether one's gift is in speaking or serving, God's grace is administered through the activity of faithful believers. The aim of the faithful steward is to give other members of the household a taste of God's grace and goodness.

We can imagine from the context and content of Peter's letter what this might mean. Believers would gather together with many of them facing enormous pressures. Some are having a hard time at work (2:18ff), some face great difficulties at home (3:1ff); others are suffering for their faith (3:14ff). Others are struggling to stand for Christ amidst enormous peer pressure (4:3ff). Finding that the Christian life is tough, they feel worn down and ready to give in. This is why they need to receive a taste of God's goodness (grace) to give them strength for the next leg of their journey.

d) Speaking (4:11a)

Some will have gifts of speaking. Their role is to give people a taste of God's goodness through their speaking by serving up a dish which contains the Word of God. Serving up their own words will not nourish and build up the flock. The sheep will only thrive on a diet containing the very words of God. Because they recognise the critical importance of what they say for the well-being of believers facing great pressures, the ones who speak must approach their role in humility.

e) Serving (4:11b)

Others will have gifts in the area of service. For example, in a contemporary setting some will welcome people into the church building, some will offer musical gifts while others make the coffee. Yet the common feature is that each should see their role as giving those who attend the meeting a taste of God's goodness as they perform their act of service. For this to happen they will certainly need to depend on God to supply the strength and energy to keep on serving all those who gather, so that it is God's name that is glorified.

No wonder the passage ends with a doxology. Peter's vision is of Christians under enormous pressure coming together in order to delight in God's grace and goodness even as they wait for Christ to appear at the end. The focus is not on the problems and trials but on God Himself who is glorified amongst His people

3) *Summary*

The pressures faced by the church may be considerable and could easily lead to despair before God, friction within the fellowship and selfish behaviour. To counter these natural tendencies Peter closes this section which began at 2:11 with a call for the church family to pray, love and serve. They are to pray, confident that God will bring about the judgment of His enemies and the salvation of believers. They are to stretch themselves in love for one another. They are to revive and strengthen weary and exhausted believers by giving them a taste of God's goodness as they minister in word and deed so that, even in difficult days, God's name is glorified.

From text to teaching

(1) *Get the message clear*

Big idea *(theme)*

The church family are to support one another in times of opposition and persecution through prayer, love and service.

Big questions *(aim)*

Preaching or teaching on this passage should answer the following questions:

+ What will help a church to pray more faithfully?
+ Why is loving one another so key to living together as God's people?
+ What is the goal of serving one another within the church family?

(2) Engage the hearer
Point of contact
In the middle of a storm out at sea it is good to hear that calmer weather is forecast. However, the crew still have to ride out the storm and that will be done only as they work together. Similarly, as believers find themselves facing a storm of opposition and persecution, it is only as they devote themselves to working together that they can ride out this storm with confidence.

Dominant picture
In darkness, our vision is restricted and so Peter is encouraging Christians to put on the equivalent of night-vision goggles. Even though surrounded by the darkness of a hostile culture, by reminding themselves of the gospel and what will happen on the day of judgment, they are able to be clear-minded about the end and this will help them to pray in a much more informed way.

(3) Application
i) Far too often it is the church prayer meeting which is least well attended. There is little urgency because there is no recognition that the day of God's judgment is drawing near. Prayer is given little priority because there are so many things to do in the busyness of our lives. As a result, our prayer meetings can be small and dull. Peter's teaching

is designed to get the church prayer meeting back on its feet. He gives us an urgency by setting it in the context of the end and the fact of the impending day of God's judgment and the limited opportunity for preaching the gospel before that day (4:5-7a). Further, he calls us to assess our lives and priorities carefully, with his call for Christians to be self-controlled and sober-minded. Taking a sober view we know God's help is vital for us individually and corporately. Therefore, the need is for us to have our lives controlled and ordered in such a way that prayer becomes a clear priority – evidenced in the commitment to pray together.

ii) The challenge for Christians is to show greater love. It is easy to love others who are generally fairly lovable. Yet so often love stops there and is unprepared to stretch further. Unspoken limits are set beyond which we dare not go. We may withdraw or look down on those who have stumbled into sin and we set severe limits into how we use our time, money and homes. The result can be a cold-hearted and grumbling community – a travesty of the church that Peter has in mind in these verses. We will need to consider what loving each other at full stretch might mean within our fellowships as we offer both forgiveness and friendship.

iii) It is easy to use gifts, which God in His grace has entrusted to us, for our personal gratification and glory. Personal jealousies and empire-building can dominate a fellowship. We need to be challenged to see how our gifts can best be used to serve others, not ourselves and as the means by which others will receive a taste of God's goodness. If we fail to serve, or if we do so in the wrong spirit or relying on our own energy, God's people will not taste anything of God's goodness. Yet if we are prepared to engage in the hard work of serving, whatever our gift, if done humbly and prayerfully, others around will receive the enormous blessing of being revived and strengthened by tasting God's goodness for themselves, so that they are equipped to go out into the next stage of their journey as believers in a hostile world.

iv) It is important to notice the stunning phrase 'whoever speaks, as one who speaks oracles of God' (4:11a ESV). We need to be reminded to treasure teaching and preaching because through human words we are hearing the very Word of God. Such words need to be listened to with a humble and teachable spirit as we recognise the enormous privilege of what is happening.

v) 'The chief end of man is to glorify God and to enjoy Him forever' (Westminster Catechism). This paragraph helps to orient the direction of our lives correctly. The overriding aim of the whole of Christian living is that God's name be glorified now and in the future (2:12; 4:11). Such an understanding is enormously refreshing and energising, as all our life becomes focused more and more in this direction.

Proclaiming the message
A preaching outline
Title: 'Living As God's People In The Light Of The End'
Text: 1 Peter 4:7-11
(1) Praying (4:7)
(2) Loving (4:8, 9)
(3) Serving (4:10, 11)

Other preaching possibilities
This paragraph might be of particular use for a church leadership considering or reviewing its ministry and activi-

ties. To what extent are Peter's priorities reflected in the life of our church family? What are the particular challenges which come from this passage that should shape the behaviour of the church family?

It might prove fruitful to gather together an overview of Peter's teaching on the church. The relevant passages would include 1:22–2:10; 3:8-12; 4:7-11 & 5:1-11. With the exception of 3:8-12 (linked to 4:7-11 as argued above), it is striking that these passages all come at the end of each of Peter's three major sections. Having set out the future privileges of God's chosen people (1:3-21), Peter describes what the church is and how it comes into being and grows (1:22–2:10). Having then set out how believers are to function within the world as exiles (2:11–3:7), Peter shows how the church is to live and function together (3:8-12; 4:7-11), especially in the light of the hostile pressures which threaten it (3:13–4:6). Peter regards the church as pivotal within God's purposes both in relation to God and in how it is to function within the world.

Leading a Bible study

Title: **'Living As God's People In The Light Of The End'**

Text: **1 Peter 4:7-11**

(1) Introduce the issues

In looking at this passage it is important to remember the context of opposition which Peter has considered since 3:13. Why does he insert a section about operating as a church family after speaking about the reality of persecution? How important is the church family when Christians are facing opposition?

(2) *Study the passage*

i)   What things about 'the end' should we be aware of from 4:5, 6 (v. 7)?

ii) According to verse 7, what factors will help us in our praying?

iii) How might Christians facing persecution or opposition (3:13–4:6) have sinned and how could the church show love in such circumstances (v. 8)?

iv) Why might Peter see the need to encourage the exercise of hospitality without grumbling (v. 9)?

v)   What is the aim of being a steward, and what does it mean to faithfully administer God's grace (v. 10 and see Luke 12:41ff)?

vi) In what ways does Peter envisage God's grace being administered to other believers (v. 11)?

vii) What is the ultimate goal of using gifts within the church family (v. 11)?

(3) *Think it through*

i)   How should our understanding of the gospel and the verdict of the final day affect our praying (v. 7)?

ii) How does failing to be self-controlled and clear-minded reveal itself in our prayer lives (v. 7)?

iii) Are there areas of your church life where there could be greater depth of love for one another (vv. 8, 9)?

iv) How is it possible to identify gifts of speaking and serving within the church family (vv. 10, 11)?

(4) *Live it out*

i)   How does this passage challenge my commitment to other church members, for example, in my participation in the church prayer gatherings?

ii) How could we encourage each other to be more prepared to use our gifts and to serve within the church
family?

16

'SUFFERING AND GLORY IN THE WORLD'

(1 PETER 4:12-19)

Peter finished Section 2 with a doxology (4:11) which could have easily formed the conclusion to the letter. Having dealt with the relationship of the Christian to God (Section 1) and to the world (Section 2), what else is there to say?

However, all the way through the letter Peter has recognised the reality of suffering (e.g. 1:6, 7; 2:20; 3:14), the importance of following Jesus' example (e.g. 2:21ff; 3:8, 9; 4:1ff) and the glorious destination awaiting the believer (e.g. 1:3ff; 1:13; 3:21ff; 4:6). He now weaves these three themes together in three final passages (4:12-19; 5:1-4; 5:5-11) to underline their importance, showing on three occasions in this final section that the normal Christian life involves sharing Christ's sufferings in the expectation of sharing Christ's glory ... and in the meantime following Christ's example. That is Peter's agenda in Section 3 which he develops in three passages; the Christian in the world (4:12-19), the Christian leader (5:1-4), and the Christian in the church (5:5-11).

Peter is not, therefore, simply rounding things off. In this final section his aim is to imprint the pattern of Christ's life (suffering leading to glory) and the example of His life on each and every believer as the fitting climax to his letter.

Listening to the text
(1) *Preliminary observations*
Peter began the second main section of his letter with 'Dear friends' (2:11) and therefore the recurrence of this phrase would appear to signal a third section. Furthermore, 4:12 follows on from a doxology (4:11) and though this does not guarantee that Peter is finishing one section, it is a strong indication that this is the case (see Rom. 11:33-36).

Many commentators simply see chapters 4 and 5 as a series of interlocking paragraphs: persecution (4:1-6) – church (4:7-11) – persecution (4:12-19) – church (5:1-11). Yet on careful inspection it can be seen that 4:12–5:11 is a distinct section with a clear theme.

With no specific reference to the Section 1 theme of hope, and, unlike Section 2, almost no reference to doing good (except at 4:19), it is clear that Section 3 has a different agenda. There is continuity, however, with both earlier sections in the references to the glory of Christ being revealed (cf. 1:7, 11, 13 and 4:13; 5:1, 4) and references to suffering.

The word 'sufferings' occurs in the plural on three occasions in section 3 – 4:13; 5:1; 5:9. Each time it refers to what believers undergo rather than what Christ underwent on the cross. Peter ties the present experience of sharing the sufferings of Christ with the prospect of His glory being revealed (4:13; 5:1, 4, 10). In other words, the pattern of Christ (suffering now with glories to follow 1:11) is to be stamped on the life of every Christian. We share His sufferings, we will share His glory.

The structure of 4:12-19 helps us to see Peter's train of thought. Verses 12 and 13 form a contrast: don't be surprised about this … but rejoice in that. These verses act as a headline, not just for the paragraph, but for the section as a whole (4:12–5:11). Verses 14-16 begin and end with a reference to the 'name' (of Christ) and explain how to respond to suffering as a Christian. Verses 17 and 18 continue the theme of explaining why Christians suffer, but also these verses bring the fate of non-Christians into the picture as well. Verse 19 forms a conclusion by indicating how, in the light of verses 12 and 13, the Christian is to continue to live.

(2) Exposition
i) The pattern of Jesus Christ (4:12, 13)
The new section begins by referring back to the trials that Peter's readers were facing (1:6, 7). The 'painful trial' probably refers to some sort of persecution, though it may still be primarily verbal rather than physical attacks which are in view (on the basis that 4:14 refers to Christians being insulted). Peter's main point is to encourage them not to be surprised that this is their current experience. He wants them to see that such events are exactly what the Christian should expect. Why should this be the case?

The answer lies in verse 13. The pattern of Jesus Christ is to be stamped on every individual believer. Just as Jesus Christ experienced sufferings followed by glories (1:11) so too will the Christian. Currently, believers will share Christ's sufferings, but they will also go on to see His glory being revealed (as at 1:5, 7, 13), which will result in believers sharing His glory (1:7). No wonder Peter encourages believers to be glad and rejoice with great joy (with echoes of 1:6, 8) because suffering as a Christian is the hallmark which proves we are on the path to seeing Christ's glory revealed.

By 'participating in Christ's sufferings', Peter does not intend any mystical understanding. He simply means that when Christians suffer because of their faith and allegiance to Jesus Christ, they are sharing His sufferings. The references to being insulted in the name of Christ (4:14) and suffering as a Christian (4:16) help to explain verse 13. Peter is not dealing with the normal types of suffering experienced by everybody in life, whatever their religion or race, he is speaking particularly of Christians who suffer due to their faith in Christ.

Although there were hints of this teaching at 1:6, 7, these verses now make it absolutely clear that the pathway to the Christian's hope of glory is through sharing Christ's sufferings. It would surely be a source of great comfort for them to hear that their experience of suffering was not out of the ordinary or surprising. Rather, it was a clear indicator that they were on the right route as they followed Christ to glory.

ii) Suffering for Christ (4:14-18)

Yet though the logic of verse 13 is straightforward (like Christ, suffering will lead to glory), Peter recognises that the very experience of suffering may cloud this picture. Those suffering for being Christians may well feel that they have actually been abandoned by God. Further, their experiences of being insulted, belittled and ridiculed may leave them feeling ashamed for holding such beliefs, and a sense of unfairness concerning those who are persecuting them – apparently with impunity. Peter recognises that for

Christians going through times of suffering these are very
pertinent issues.

a) The suffering Christian and God – where is He? (4:14)
To the person who feels completely abandoned by God
when ridiculed and insulted for his faith in Christ, there is
a repetition of the teaching from the Sermon on the Mount
(Matt. 5:10-12), which Peter has already used at 3:14.
Though the believer may feel cursed, such a person is in fact
blessed. This is an objective statement which is true for the
believer regardless of his feelings or situation. He is blessed
by God and this is reinforced in one of the most remarkable
statements within the letter. Though the revelation of Jesus
Christ's glory awaits the final day to which believers look
forward with joyful anticipation (4:13), nevertheless, even
now, they are told that 'the Spirit of glory and of God rests
on you'. This image picks up the Old Testament theme of
God's glory hovering over God's people in their wilderness
journeys but also the specific reference to the Spirit of the
Lord resting upon the messianic figure of Isaiah 11:1, 2.
Even as the Spirit of glory rested on God's people in the
past and on Jesus Christ, so He rests on the believers even
as they go through painful trials and suffering. Rather than
suffering clouding the believer's current experience of God,
it is a sign of God's glorious presence with them. As the
believer shares in Christ's sufferings he even now shares
in His privileges whilst looking forward to future glory.
He can therefore also have full assurance of the present
help of the Spirit in times of persecution, as promised by
Jesus Christ (see Matt. 10:20). In other words, though the
Christian may feel completely cut off from God, the reality
is that God has not abandoned him and is far closer (resting
on him!) than he could possibly imagine.

b) The suffering Christian and himself (4:15, 16)

Peter reiterates an earlier theme (2:20; 3:17), reminding the person who may feel ashamed by insults that he would have every reason to feel that way if his suffering is due to his own sinful behaviour. It is striking that Peter includes in verse 15 not only references to obvious sins but also to being a 'meddler' or interfering busybody. However, if his suffering is not due to such reasons, but instead is caused by his allegiance to Christ, then Peter states that there is no need to be ashamed (2:6 and the contrast in 3:16). The believer is incredibly privileged to have been called by Christ and to bear His name as he represents Him in the world. If he is persecuted for the very reason that he is seeking to serve Christ then he is to remind himself of the privilege, however great the cost may be.

c) The suffering Christian and his non-Christian persecutors
  (4:17, 18)

To the person suffering for his faith in Christ and aware of the contrast between himself and his persecutors, Peter has a different message. He may well be feeling that life is completely unfair – he is persecuted and even martyred, whilst his persecutors live prosperous lives and die peacefully in their beds surrounded by their family and friends. Peter's response is first to remind them that their suffering is not arbitrary nor ultimately in the hands of their persecutors. Rather it is part of God's sovereign, eternal purposes whereby He sends and uses suffering to refine the church (cf. 1:6, 7; 4:12 and for Old Testament examples see Ezek. 9:6; Mal. 3:1-5) so that the dross is removed and the genuine article of faith in Christ can be seen clearly. Second, Peter also brings assurance to suffering believers by reminding them of the future. They are to look at the eventual outcome of all things rather than let their thoughts be dominated by the current situation. They are to keep a future perspective not only for their own lives (4:13) but also for the lives of those who do not obey the gospel (cf. 2:8; 3:1; 3:20). The apparently rhetorical questions in 4:17, 18 recall the promise in 2:8 that when the final day comes and the Lord Jesus Christ is revealed, these people are in for a calamitous fall.

In verses 14-18 Peter is responding to the very real concerns that suffering Christians would be experiencng and his aim is to provide encouragement and assurance through giving them new perspectives on their trials. God is with them. They are privileged to bear Christ's name. Their enemies will not escape God's judgment at the end.

(iii) The example of Jesus Christ (4:19)

Peter's 'So then' or 'Therefore' (ESV) indicates a conclusion to this passage. His big idea is that Christians must understand the pattern of Jesus Christ as being normative – sufferings now with glories to follow. Yet how should this affect their ongoing life amidst their sufferings? Peter's response is that those who suffer according to God's will and purpose must keep on following Christ as their example by doing two things:

First, Christians are to entrust their souls to a faithful Creator. This is exactly what Jesus did in His sufferings on the cross (cf. 2:23) and Christians are to follow His example. Perhaps the reason Peter uses this unusual description of God is to highlight that, as the Creator of all, He is in complete control of all that happens within His creation, as the Lord Jesus teaches in Matthew 10:29-31. He can be trusted to know exactly what Christians are going through in their times of suffering.

Second, Christians are to continue to do good. Clearly
this picks up on a very prominent theme in Section 2
(2:11–4:11), but should also be recognised as an important
characteristic of Jesus' earthly life. In Peter's sermon before
Cornelius he described Jesus Christ's ministry as, 'He went
around doing good and healing all who were under the
power of the devil, because God was with him' (Acts 10:38).
For Christians to continue to do good is therefore another
aspect of following Jesus Christ's example.

(3) *Summary*

In this new section Peter draws together his earlier teaching
by providing a simple framework for Christians living amidst
hostility. They are to embrace the pattern of Jesus Christ's
life (suffering followed by glories), confident that present
suffering is not a sign of their abandonment by God, but
of preparation for the glories to come, and so follow Jesus
Christ as their example.

From text to teaching

(1) *Get the message clear*

Big idea (theme)

The pattern of Jesus Christ's experience (sufferings now
followed by glories later) is to be stamped on the life of all
believers as they follow Christ.

Big questions (aim)

Preaching or teaching on this passage should answer the
following questions:

+ Why should believers not think it strange that they
   suffer as Christians?

+ How should this pattern provide encouragements for suffering Christians?

+ How should the example of Christ be shown in their everyday lives?

(2) Engage the hearer
Point of contact
In unfamiliar surroundings, it is easy to get disorientated and be unsure whether you have taken the correct route. Peter's readers are tempted to look at the suffering which they are experiencing as signs that somewhere they must have taken the wrong road. Peter's aim is to reassure them that they are actually on the right track, since Jesus Christ went the same way.

Dominant picture
A young child is coping with a serious illness in hospital. Naturally, the parents stay close by the bed all through the night, never drifting far away. Though the youngster is not always aware of them, they are as close as it is possible for them to be. In verse 14 Peter is seeking to encourage embattled and suffering believers with the assurance that they have not been abandoned by God. Far from it – God is closer than they could possibly imagine, resting on them by His Spirit.

(3) Application
i) Suffering is generally regarded as something which must be avoided at all costs. It is not easy to keep a proper perspective concerning God's purposes when we are in the midst of suffering but it is vital. Unbelievers think it 'strange' that believers don't plunge into sinful behaviour precisely

because they cannot see future judgment coming (4:4, 5). The believer, on the other hand, should not think times of testing as 'strange' as they are indicative of a glorious future (12, 13). Present experiences are not strange once set in the wider context of where they lead.

ii) The response Peter is looking for is not tight-lipped determination but joy. Clearly this is not a joy produced through ignoring the suffering, but solidly rooted in a proper theological understanding of the situation we are in. Though others may insult and ridicule us, God has blessed us and He is preparing to bring us to glory. The preacher cannot command Christians who suffer to be joyful but it is vital that he lays the theological foundation properly, so that when those who hear him do suffer for their faith, they have the resources to see how this actually confirms their privileged status as God's people, which should lead to joy.

iii) We need to remind Christians that though insulted and dismissed by non-Christians, God's verdict is more important. If He blesses, then ultimately the curses of men have no effect. If His Spirit rests on the believer then however isolated and weak he may feel, he is in fact known and loved.

iv) Although 4:17, 18 is intended to reassure believers, it does so by way of contrasting the fate of those who do not obey the gospel of God. These verses therefore constitute a warning to the non-Christian. The challenge is to lift the unbelievers' gaze to the future in order to persuade them to obey God now.

v) Jesus Christ is the model for every Christian to copy. A Christ-like life is what Peter seeks in this passage and elsewhere in this epistle, perhaps reflecting the teaching he heard from the lips of Jesus Christ, 'If anyone would come after me, he must deny himself and take up His cross and follow me' (Mark 8:34).

Proclaiming the message
A preaching outline
Title: **'Suffering And Glory In The World'**
Text: **1 Peter 4:12-19**
(1) The pattern of Jesus Christ (12, 13)
(2) Suffering for Christ (14-18)
(3) The example of Jesus Christ (19)

Other preaching possibilities

Having seen that the pattern of Christ (suffering now with glories to follow) is evident in each of the three parts of Section 3 (4:12–5:11), it would be straightforward to preach the whole section in one go, dipping into each of the passages as time permits:

A.	We share Christ's sufferings	4:12-18	5:1	5:8, 9
B.	We will share Christ's glory	4:13	5:1, 4	5:10, 11
C.	We keep following Christ	4:19	5:2, 3	5:5-7

Even if the preacher feels that this will involve too much material for one sermon, it may be that such an outline could introduce this section of the letter.

It might be a useful exercise to gather together references to the treatment that some Christians were receiving in Peter's day (cf. 4:14). These will include accusations of doing wrong (2:12), ignorant talk about Christians (2:15), insults (3:9), malicious and frightening threats (3:14, 16), personal abuse for not joining in sinful activity (4:4) and further insults for being a follower of Christ (4:14). At times this may be linked with questioning which may be friendly, but could well be hostile (3:15). Depicting this background and recognising the links with contemporary situations could be extremely helpful in enabling people to see the relevance of 1 Peter to their own situation.

Leading a Bible study

Title: 'Suffering And Glory In The World'

Text: **1 Peter 4:12-19**

(1) Introduce the issues

What realistic advice might you give to someone about to enter a marathon race or embark on climbing a mountain? In what ways is Peter's opening advice in verse 12 similar?

(2) Study the passages

i)   Why should believers not be surprised by suffering as Christians (vv. 12, 13)?

ii) On what basis can Peter encourage suffering Christians to rejoice (v. 13)?

iii) What does God's blessing consist of in verse 14?

iv) What are the reasons for Christians not to be ashamed of suffering? When should they be ashamed (vv. 14-16)?

v)   What message do verses 17, 18 bring to those who are doing the persecuting ... and to those who are being persecuted?

vi) How should Christians respond when suffering comes, according to verse 19?

(3) Think it through

i)   In what way is the whole of our Christian life simply a matter of following Christ (vv. 12, 13)?

ii)   What does it mean to bear Christ's name and how should this be an encouragement to us (vv. 14-16)?

iii) In what ways does knowing the outcome or the ending help us to keep things in perspective (see vv. 13, 17, 18)?

iv)   How does verse 19 help suffering Christians who might have been on the verge of giving up?

(4) *Live it out*

i)   How could joy become a more dominant feature of our lives as Christians?

ii)   How does this passage help us to support and pray for the suffering church throughout the world?

17

'SUFFERING AND GLORY IN CHRISTIAN LEADERSHIP'

(1 PETER 5:1-4)

The pattern of present suffering leading to future glory (see 4:13) is now applied to the leaders of the church.

Christian leaders are also to embrace the example of Christ in the way in which they exercise their ministries. As they reflect the example of the Good Shepherd, so they fulfil their ministry of being shepherds to God's flock.

Listening to the text

(1) Preliminary observations

In line with the overall thrust of Section 3 of the letter (4:12–5:11), Peter speaks of the reality of sharing in the sufferings of Christ, before seeing His glory revealed (see 5:1 and 4:13; 5:10, 11).

Since 'glory' comes at verse 1 and the end of verse 4, it seems preferable to deal with 5:1-4 as a separate unit. 'Glory' is now not only something to be revealed through Christ, but also to be received or experienced by the believer.

Some commentators see a connection between 5:1-4 and 4:17 and note that judgment on the household of God starts with the elders at Ezekiel 9:6. The background there, however, was the elders' idolatry, and there are probably other factors at play here. In a context where the church is being persecuted and going through a 'painful trial' it is often church leaders who will be most exposed to suffering. In such a situation it may not be surprising that some leaders would be unwilling to lead (cf. 5:2). Given that Peter knows from first-hand experience what it is like to be targeted as a Christian leader (e.g. Acts 12:1-5), he deals specifically with the need to encourage such leaders before turning his attention to the whole church family in the remainder of the letter (5:5-11).

(2) Exposition
i) Elders share in Christ's sufferings (5:1)
There is a variety of terms used within the passage referring to the elders. They are literally older men, presumably drawn from within the congregation, (in contrast to the young men mentioned later at 5:5). They are also given the job of being shepherds (5:2) and have a ministry involving the exercise of oversight (from which Greek word we have 'episcopal' designating the ministry of a bishop). In this early setting the terms elder, shepherd (or its derivative, pastor) and bishop seem to be interchangeable and overlap in their range of meaning. Similar terms are used at Acts 20:17, 28 and Titus 1:6, 7 (where the job of providing oversight is to be done by elders).

To these elders, Peter, an apostle of Jesus Christ (1:1), identifies himself as a fellow elder. His ministry is largely the same as theirs. As with all the elders and other believers,

Peter is to be a sharer in the glory that is to be revealed. Given this reference, it is likely that what Peter says about the sufferings of Christ is also something shared with other believers. Some argue that Peter is referring to his own eyewitness experience of Jesus' sufferings on the cross. However, Peter's use of the plural for 'sufferings', as at 4:13, suggests that he has in view the experiences of church members (and here, church leaders) as they suffer for their allegiance to Christ. In his own experience as an apostle and elder he has been a witness (literally a martyr) to the sufferings of Christ, i.e. the sufferings which came to Christ's people through their allegiance to His name. (See, for example, Acts 4:3; 5:18 and 12:3.)

Peter is therefore hammering home from his own experiences the normative framework for all Christians established at 4:13 but now applied to Christian leaders at 5:1. The pattern of Christ is stamped on every believer and Christian leaders are no exception – first there is suffering and then there is glory. First comes the cross and then the crown (see 5:4). Not only is there no immunity to suffering in Christian leadership, but such suffering should be expected and recognised not as a sign of abandonment by God, but a confirmation of authentic leadership.

Verse 1 functions then as a word of reassurance to suffering church leaders that their suffering, as with Peter's, is a mark of authentic Christian experience on the journey to glory.

ii) *Elders are to shepherd the flock by following Christ's example*
     (5:2, 3)

The role of leaders is to follow the example of Jesus Christ. He has already been introduced at 2:25 as the Shepherd and Overseer (episkopos) to whom they have returned, and elders are to shepherd the flock which belongs to God and exercise a ministry of oversight (5:2).

Of course Peter would have been familiar with Jesus speaking of Himself as a shepherd (see Mark 14:27 and John 10:1-18). He would also have remembered his own personal commissioning by the risen Jesus in John 21:15-17, where he is given the job of feeding and taking care of the lambs and sheep.

Peter now highlights three distinctive features of what this will involve.

a) Do the job willingly ... not under compulsion (5:2)

In the context of opposition and persecution (see 4:12ff) elders might be reluctant to serve because of the physical dangers involved. Such an unwilling leader might be tempted to alleviate any suffering by complying with the authorities in watering down the faith or deserting the flock. The flock needs a shepherd who will follow Jesus Christ's example and be willing to suffer for the sake of the flock (cf. John 10:11-15). The Good Shepherd was not under compulsion, but acted willingly and voluntarily to save the sheep whatever the personal cost (cf. John 10:18). That is the attitude which Peter longs to see within the under-shepherds of Christ's flock. Their ministry should be driven not by what is set out in a job description, but from a willingness before God to serve His sheep.

b) Do the job eagerly ... not for financial gain (5:2)

Peter now uses a term which was also used by Paul (see 1 Tim. 3:8; Titus 1:7) and relates to financial greed. Both agree that those involved in Christian leadership should not be motivated by issues of financial reward. Such a mindset would easily lead to very grudging ministry where the focus is on what the minister receives rather than on what the flock requires. The Good Shepherd contrasts with the hired hand who cares more for his salary than the well-being and safety of the sheep (cf. John 10:11-13). Within 5:1-4 there is the stark contrast between those who seek earthly rewards (such as money and status) and those who receive a glorious heavenly reward (the crown of glory 5:4). Peter longs to see eager service whether the salary is adequate or non-existent. He longs to see a changed mindset where the focus is not on the minister but on the ministry.

c). Do the job lovingly … not for personal status (5:3)
Sacrificial service is contrasted to the exercise of forceful authority. Peter recognised that it would be an easy step for those given authority within the flock to abuse the power that they had been given and start throwing their weight around, acting like the false shepherds of Ezekiel 34 or the Gentile rulers who 'lord it over them' (Mark 10:41-45, with the same word as at 1 Peter 5:3). The elders are to be examples to the flock by following Jesus' example, seeking to serve rather than be served. The cross is not only to be proclaimed by word but demonstrated in the lives of the elders, so that the flock both hears and sees the gospel.

It is an enormous privilege for elders to be involved in serving the flock that is owned by God in this way. However, they are not to see themselves as overall in charge since they are to function under a Chief Shepherd (5:4). As Peter himself was commissioned, their most important roles would be to feed the flock (presumably with God's Word 2:2) and to protect it from danger. The Good Shepherd's example is to be paramount.

iii) Elders will share in Christ's glory (5:4)

The day when the Lord Jesus Christ is revealed in all His glory (1:5, 7, 13; 4:13) is also the day when the Christian shares in that glory: a thought now developed at the end of this passage. At His first appearing Jesus came as a lamb (cf. 1:19, 20; 2:22f), but at His final appearing He will come as the Chief Shepherd. Though there are 'rewards' which are inappropriate for elders to seek in this life (cf. 5:2, 3), there is a glorious crown awaiting them on that day. All believers will receive honour and glory (cf. 1:7), but included within this is a particular encouragement to the elders that their labour has not been in vain. As part of the inheritance which is imperishable and unfading (1:4) there is to be an unfading crown of glory presented to them. This is to be the focus of their ministry rather than any earthly rewards.

(3) Summary

Christians involved in leadership are to be encouraged that authentic Christian experience is present suffering leading to future glory as they continue to lead the church even through very difficult days. They will aim to do their job of shepherding God's flock by following the costly and sacrificial example of the Good Shepherd, Jesus Christ.

From text to teaching

(1) Get the message clear

Big idea (theme)

Christian leaders are to follow the pattern and example of Jesus Christ as they fulfil their ministry.

Big questions (aim)

Preaching or teaching on this passage should answer the following questions:

- In what ways should the example of Jesus the Good Shepherd be a model for Christian leaders?
- What are the things which should motivate Christian leaders in their service of Christ?
- What does it mean to be a witness of Christ's sufferings?

(2) *Engage the hearer*
Point of contact

Being a church leader – visible to the outside world – in a context of persecution and opposition is a risky business. It is often the church leader who is the first to be arrested or martyred. No wonder Peter has to deal with the situation of pastors who were unwilling to find themselves in this sort of situation.

Dominant picture

Some of us will be used to handling money and making decisions about where to invest. We want a good return on our savings and the main question in our minds is, what's in it for me? However, that mindset is fatal in Christian ministry. The Good Shepherd is asking, what's in it for them?

(3) *Application*

i) It is important, both for the church family and for those in pastoral leadership, to be clear what the 'job description' of a Christian leader is. As elders, who have a certain degree of maturity in the Christian faith and standing within the local church family, they operate as shepherds and overseers. They reflect Jesus' ministry (2:25) and are, under God, part of the means by which Jesus Christ currently exercises His ongoing ministry through the church. As shepherds they have the responsibility of feeding the flock with God's Word. As those exercising oversight they have responsibility for souls (2:25) achieving their goal of salvation on the day when Jesus Christ is revealed (see 1:9). The spiritual responsibility of caring for the flock by building them up and ensuring that they are not diverted needs to be the focus for Christian leaders in the local church.

ii) If Peter suffered as an elder then it is unlikely that those who take on the same role will be immune to suffering. This needs to be recognised, so that Christian leaders are not surprised when suffering comes their way, and church members will want to support their leaders, recognising the pressures of their work.

iii) It is striking that both for Peter and also for Paul (e.g. 1 Tim. 3:1ff) most of the qualifications for church leadership relate to issues of character and lifestyle. Preaching the Lord Jesus Christ is to be done not just with our lips but with our lives. The message of Jesus Christ will not be commended if the lifestyle of the leader is not also pointing in the same direction. Though Christian leaders will always fall short of the ideal, nevertheless the pattern of the cross, with loving, sacrificial service at its heart, will commend itself powerfully to any church family (and surely the love of the church family for their pastor should cover over any of his shortcomings – cf. 4:8). On the other hand, where pastors have selfishly put their own interests first and used their authority to bully members of God's flock, there is likely to be considerable difficulty as well as serious misunderstanding of the gospel.

iv) Though the cost of Christian leadership can be considerable, the rewards are amazing. Seeing and meeting the Chief Shepherd and receiving the unfading crown from His hand will surely put all the hardships and struggles of ministry into perspective. Though Paul states that the crown will be given 'to all who have longed for His appearing' (2 Tim. 4:8), nevertheless Peter's focus on the reward to be received by the elders is a word of reassurance to encourage them in their ministries. As is typical of Peter, he encourages us to have a future perspective in everything. To be of earthly use we will need to be heavenly minded.

Proclaiming the message
A preaching outline

Title: 'Suffering And Glory In Christian Leadership'
Text: 1 Peter 5:1-4
(1) Elders share in Christ's sufferings (5:1)
(2) Elders are to shepherd the flock by following Christ's example (5:2, 3)
(3) Elders will share in Christ's glory (5:4)

Other preaching possibilities
As it is slightly unclear where to divide 5:1-11 (after v. 4 as above, v. 5a or even v. 5) it may be that the preacher would want to incorporate 5:1-11 into one sermon:
(1) Church leaders (5:1-4)
  i.   suffering (5:1)
  ii.   following Christ as a shepherd (5:2, 3)
  iii. glory (5:1, 4)
(2) Church members (5:5-11)
  i.   suffering (5:8, 9)
  ii.   following Christ in humility (5:5-7)
  iii. glory (5:10, 11)

This is the only passage in 1 Peter which deals directly with church leadership. Bearing in mind that 5:1-4 needs to be kept within its context, nevertheless it would provide a good study for any leadership group within the local church or ministers' fraternal. Another possibility would be to build on the 'shepherd' theme, also using Ezekiel 34 and John 10:

(1) *Ezekiel 34 – what are the hallmarks of a false shepherd?*

(2) *John 10:11-18 – what are the hallmarks of a good shepherd?*

(3) *1 Peter 5:1-4 – what is the chief Shepherd looking for in His under-shepherds?*

Leading a Bible study

Title: **'Suffering And Glory In Christian Leadership'**

Text: **1 Peter 5:1-4**

(1) Introduce the issues

What are the main characteristics which the world values in leaders? To what extent should we want these characteristics in church leaders?

(2) Study the passage

   i)   In what ways is Peter a model to the elders to whom he writes ... and how is Peter's life modelled on Christ's (v. 1)?

   ii) What are the particular dangers and temptations that Peter highlights in verses 2 and 3 to which the elders might be prone?

   iii) In each of these areas, how does Peter encourage the elders or shepherds to imitate the Good Shepherd (vv. 2 and 3 and John 10:11-18)?

   iv) To whom does the flock belong and how much value is placed upon it (v. 2 and Acts 20:28)?

v) What rewards can the faithful shepherd look forward to (v. 4)?

(3) *Think it through*

i) In what ways is it so easy for church leaders to have the mentality of the hireling (John 10:11ff) rather than the Good Shepherd?

ii) Why is Peter so concerned about the character of the elders rather than about their ability to handle God's Word (vv. 2 and 3)?

iii) What would be the danger of having a superb Bible teacher who nevertheless fell into the traps mentioned in verses 2 and 3?

(4) *Live it out*

i) What are the ways you could best support, encourage and pray for your church leaders to fulfil the pattern outlined in these verses?

ii) How does this passage encourage us to take the pattern of following Christ more seriously?

18

'SUFFERING AND GLORY IN THE CHURCH'

(1 PETER 5:5-11)

In this final passage Peter rounds off his teaching by weaving together the three themes which have been so prominent in Section three (4:12–5:11). Church members are to follow Jesus by embracing His example of humility and prayerful dependence. They are to embrace the sufferings of Christ by standing firm against the devil, and they can look forward confidently 'after a little while' to sharing Christ's eternal glory, fully restored after their time of suffering. In every way Jesus' experience brings together not only clear guidelines concerning how to live but also much comfort concerning the future.

Listening to the text
(1) Preliminary observations
i) In this passage, Peter moves the suffering/glory teaching to the end in order to leave the reader with this ringing in his ears (see 5:9-11). It should be noted that 'sufferings' occurs in the plural (5:9) as at 1:11, 4:13 and 5:1 and 'glory'

has been an even stronger theme at the end of the book than earlier in the letter (see 4:13, 14; 5:1, 4 and 5:10).

ii) Peter ends each of his main sections with teaching which relates to how the Christian family is to operate together (see 1:22–2:10; 4:7-11; 5:5-11). The brotherhood (5:9 ESV) links with Peter's earlier focus on brotherly love (see 1:22; 2:17; 3:8).

iii) One of the important themes within this passage is humility. It occurs three times in quick succession in verses 5 and 6. Earlier, at 3:8-12, the humble Christian could expect the Lord to be attentive to their cry (3:8, 12) and a similar thought is evident at 5:5-7 with the humble Christian assured of God's care. There are parallels with James 4:6-10 which also includes the same Old Testament quotation and speaks of the reality of the devil's activity (cf. 1 Pet. 5:8).

iv) Although in a different order, the themes of suffering/ glory and following Christ are all present as in other parts of section 3 (4:12–5:11) and shape the structure of this passage. First, Peter describes the submissive life as being a life marked by humility before others and God, trusting Him to care and provide (5-7). Second, Peter introduces the theme of sufferings, this time caused by the activity of the devil (8, 9). Third, suffering will be followed by glory, ending as at 4:11 with a brief doxology (10, 11).

(2) Exposition
i) Following Jesus' example (1:5-7)
Having set out the responsibilities of the elders (5:1-4) Peter turns to the rest of the church family. In contrast to the leaders who are literally the older men, Peter first briefly addresses the 'younger men' who are to submit to their leaders (5a) before turning his attention to the whole

church. The common theme is the need for all church members (and perhaps especially the young men) to exhibit humility.

As the church leaders are to follow Jesus Christ's example in shepherding the flock so the church members are to follow Jesus Christ's example in clothing themselves with humility. At the Last Supper, Jesus exhibited humility by literally clothing Himself with a towel and washing the feet of the disciples (John 13:1-4ff), notably confident that He would return to the Father (John 13:1, 4) and in the midst of the activity of the devil (John 13:2). Similarly, Peter commends humility, confident that God will lift the believer up to be with Him in due time (5:5, 6) even in the midst of the devil's activity (5:8).

The Old Testament quotation, taken from Proverbs 3:34, is also used in James 4:6-10. Peter is not so much attacking pride within the church family as giving assurance of God's grace to those who do follow Jesus Christ in walking in humility. Grace is generally linked to the undeserved salvation which the Christian can expect to receive from God in the future (see 1:10, 13). This may well be the meaning here, since God will lift up the believer (5:6) in 'a little while' (5:10), which corresponds to the reference at 1:6, 7 and points to the day when Jesus Christ is revealed.

As by Jesus on the night before He died, humility will be evidenced in both practical service to others and a willingness to accept God's will even if it might involve suffering, both of which are evident in 5:5-7. Humility before men will involve willing service and submission; humility before God will involve prayerful trust and confidence in His care and ultimate protection (5:7). Peter presents the example of Jesus facing the same situation as his readers, which therefore speaks powerfully to encourage them to follow His example of humility.

ii) Following Jesus in suffering (5:8, 9)
As Peter turns to the reality of their present sufferings, there is a similar feel to the statement at 4:12 that believers should not be surprised at suffering, with the reminder that Christians all around the world are going through exactly the same sorts of experiences (5:9).

This time suffering comes not so much from the hostility of the world (cf. 4:14) but from the activity of the devil, who is likened to a roaring lion who aims to devour believers. Though this could refer either to the activity of the devil in tempting Christians to deny the faith or lead them into sin, it also has the flavour of physical suffering and martyrdom. Paul speaks of being delivered from the lion's mouth when he was on trial before the Gentile/Roman authorities (2 Tim. 4:16-18). Although the passages are distinct, the idea of the devil stirring up the Roman authorities against the believers is certainly a possible understanding of the text. Furthermore, there is the link with Rome through the use of 'Babylon' as a code word (5:13) for the hostile place of exile for believers (cf. Jer. 51:34 for Babylon devouring God's people).

In this situation where the devil is at work, Christians are to be sober-minded or self-controlled (5:8) as previously instructed (1:13; 4:7) and they are to be watchful. Peter passes on to his readers the mindset Jesus Christ encouraged of His disciples in facing the attacks of the devil, alert to their own weakness (Mark 14:38).

To resist the devil the believer must keep trusting God. Such behaviour will not grant immunity from suffering, since it is the experience of believers throughout the world that these sufferings 'are being accomplished' in them. This strange phrase points to God's sovereignty, indicating that their sufferings are not a matter of chance but have a place within God's overall purposes, similar to the experience of Jesus Christ in His sufferings (cf. 1:11). Though Peter denied Christ three times in order to avoid suffering, he now recognises that the right way to respond is to stand firm and trust God whatever consequences follow.

iii) Following Jesus to glory (5:10, 11)

Through God's grace the believers' everyday experience of sufferings will eventually lead to glory. 'God's mighty hand', which will lift up believers (5:6), is especially linked to the deliverance God provided for His chosen people as He prepared to take them to the Promised Land and plant them there (Exod. 3:19f; 6:1; 13:3, 9, 14, 16; 15:16ff). It is an appropriate phrase, therefore, in a letter which has made so many references to Christians as God's chosen people (see 1:1; 2:9 and 5:13). 'In due time' (5:6) links with the suffering which will last 'a little while' (5:10 and 1:6, 7) and points to the period before the revelation of Jesus Christ. When this period ends, the God who is full of grace will bring believers to glory.

The call of Christians from darkness to light (2:9) was also a call to live holy lives reflecting the example of Jesus Christ (1:15; 2:21; 3:9) and to share in Christ's glory (5:1, 10). Peter looks forward to the day when believers who have suffered considerably will enter that state, restored, confirmed, strengthened and established. 'Restored' is the term used of the nets mended by the disciples (Mark 1:19) – surely a powerful image for Peter the fisherman. 'Establish'(ESV) speaks of being securely placed on a foundation, suggesting a link with the new temple which God is building on the cornerstone of Christ (see 2:4-6). Together the phrase speaks of permanence and security, providing reassurance that the inheritance to which they look forward (1:4, 5) will indeed be imperishable.

No wonder Peter ends with a second doxology (cf. 4:11) acknowledging God's eternal power, which will safely deliver believers through suffering to glory. His mighty power (5:6, 11) will achieve all His gracious purposes (5:7, 10).

(3) *Summary*

Reinforcing the main themes of section 3 (4:12–5:11) believers are called to follow Jesus each step of their journey. They are to follow Him through Maundy Thursday as they show humility and prayerful dependence. They are to follow Him through Good Friday as they stand firm for what they believe, even though it entails suffering. Finally they are to look forward to following Jesus to the resurrection glory of Easter Day, fully restored through God's grace and power.

From text to teaching

(1) *Get the message clear*

Big idea (theme)

Christians are to keep following the pattern of Jesus Christ all the way through suffering to glory.

Big questions (aim)

Preaching or teaching on this passage should answer the following questions:

- How is humility shown before others and God?
- How does Jesus give us a model for resisting the devil?
- What should be the confident expectation of every believer?

(2) Engage the hearer

Point of contact

Many people are making use of satnav technology for their cars, in order to be assured of getting to their destination safely without getting lost en route. Christians are to navigate their way to glory, not through the latest technological breakthrough, but through fully embracing the pattern of Christ in their own lives.

Dominant picture

Clothing styles go in an out of fashion with alarming rapidity. What is 'in' one year is hopelessly out of date only a few months later. For the Christian, we find that the characteristics with which Jesus clothed Himself are always in fashion in God's eyes. Clothing ourselves with humility may not turn heads in the world, but it is essential clothing for the believer.

(3) Application

i) Our natural tendency is to consider our own needs first and to put a higher value on our own thoughts than the views of others, even if they have been put in authority over us within the church. It is against this that we need to hear Peter's encouragement to follow Jesus Christ's example of humility. If He was prepared to clothe Himself with the towel of humble service to serve His faltering disciples, how much more should we be prepared to be recognised by Christ-like humble service as we care for one another.

ii) Humble service should go hand in hand with humble acceptance of God's will, which is shown in casting our (understandable) anxieties and concerns on to Him. As Jesus cast His anxieties on to His Father in Gethsemane, so we are encouraged by Peter to do the same, confident of His care, which will ensure we will be lifted up (5:6) even if first there are sufferings to undergo. Interestingly, Peter uses the word 'cast', which as a fisherman would convey the idea of his nets being thrown into the sea in a very deliberate way. In the same way, we are to deliberately 'cast' our anxieties on God.

iii) Peter lifts up the eyes of his readers to what other Christians are going through. Finding out what is happening amongst the Christian family across the world highlights the fact that suffering for the gospel is a normal experience and helps us to fulfil Peter's instructions at 3:8 to be sympathetic, compassionate and full of brotherly love.

iv) We need to be aware of the reality and danger of the devil. However, Peter's advice seems counter-intuitive. He encourages us not to run away, denying the faith as he had done when Jesus had been arrested. Instead he requires us to stand firm and accept the consequences, trusting God to care for us in the suffering which may follow, recognising that this is exactly what many believers have to do around the world. The focus is not on the devil, or any special prayers or rites to defend against him, but on being alert and keeping a steady trust in God.

v) To people who have gone through enormous suffering for the gospel the promises of 5:10 will be very precious indeed. As a fisherman patiently mends his ripped nets such that they are perfect once again, so the Lord Jesus will perfectly restore His church ripped apart by suffering. The building that has been rocked by storms will one day be seen to be utterly secure, as believers find themselves welcomed into their new home with God forever.

vi) Peter wants Christians to be fully assured of God's grace and power which will bring us to share Christ's glory at the end. Though there is a delay between now and then, we can have complete confidence in the God of all grace whose power is for ever and ever. Arrival at this glorious destination is entirely in His hands and we are to be confident that what He has done for Christ (1:11, 21) He will do for all who are 'in Christ' (5:10, 14). This perspective is to strengthen us amidst our sufferings as we follow Jesus Christ now.

Proclaiming the message
A preaching outline

Title: **'Suffering And Glory In The Church'**
Text: **1 Peter 5:5-11**
(1) Following Jesus' example (5:5-7)
(2) Following Jesus in suffering (5:8, 9)
(3) Following Jesus to glory (5:10, 11)

Other preaching possibilities

As mentioned in previous chapters, section 3 as a whole (4:12–5:11) exhibits a clear structure in each of its three parts. 5:5-11 could be taught with the whole section (4:12–5:11) or simply with 5:1-4 using this framework:

A.	The reality of sharing in Christ's sufferings	(4:12-18)	5:1	5:8, 9
B.	The promise of sharing in Christ's glory	(4:13)	5:1, 4	5:10, 11
C.	The ongoing need to follow Christ's example	(4:19)	5:2, 3	5:5-7

Peter inserts his teaching about the church at the end of each of his sections. Gathering together this material may provide a useful framework for a short series on the church:

(1) How God's church starts and grows (1:22–2:3)
(2) How God's church relates to God (2:4-10)
(3) How God's church relates to one another (4:7-11)
(4) How God's church should be led (5:1-4)
(5) How God's church relates to the future (5:5-11)

Leading a Bible study

Title: 'Suffering And Glory In The Church'
Text: 1 Peter 5:5-11

(1) Introduce the issues

What are the things which seem to hinder your progress in the Christian life?

(2) Study the passage

   i)   How is humility to be shown within the church family (v. 5)?

   ii)   How is humility to be shown towards God (vv. 6, 7)?

   iii) In what ways does Peter envisage the devil attacking believers (vv. 8, 9)?

   iv)   How is the devil to be resisted (vv. 8, 9)?

   v)   In the context of Christians suffering around the world, why can believers have confidence in God (vv. 9-11)?

   vi)   What does God promise to do for believers, especially those who have suffered (vv. 10, 11)?

(3) Think it through

   i)   Why do we find acting humbly before others and God so difficult? (vv. 5-7)?

   ii)   What does this passage teach us about God's character and how should this be a means of great comfort and encouragement (vv. 5-11)?

iii) In what ways does our glorious destination help us to get things in perspective (vv. 6, 10, 11)?

(4) Live it out

i) How does this passage help us to cope with the difficulties we face in our Christian pilgrimage?

ii) How should the example of Christ make a bigger impact on our lives as believers?

19

'JESUS CHRIST IN 1 PETER'

Sometimes it is worth drawing together verses on a particular theme and no more important theme can be found in 1 Peter than that of the person and work of the Lord Jesus Christ. Care will need to be taken not to unload a full systematic theology on to the theme, and this sort of approach is more safely done once the preacher has been able to study the whole letter so that the context determines the meaning of individual passages and verses. Nonetheless, it can be very helpful in revealing the theological underpinning of the letter and in providing a focus for our devotion and discipleship.

Listening to the text
(1) Preliminary observations
A number of prominent themes appear in 1 Peter:
- The blood and the death of Christ 1:2, 19; 2:24; 3:18
- Response to Christ: – obedience 1:2 (1:14, 22)
  – love 1:8
  – trust 1:8; 2:6

- Resurrection of Christ   1:3, 21; 3:18, 21f
- Revelation of Jesus Christ 1:7, 13; 4:13; 5:1, 4
- Spirit of Christ   1:11
- Sufferings of Christ and subsequent glories
                            1:11, 21; 4:13; 5:1, 10f
- Titles of the living Christ – Stone   2:4
                              – Shepherd   2:25
                              – Overseer   2:25
                              – Lord   3:15
- Example of Christ in His suffering   2:21ff; 4:1
- Victory of Christ over evil   3:18-22

(2) *Exposition*

Right at the start of the letter Peter highlights two aspects of our relationship with Christ. On the one hand, the reference to the sprinkling of His blood which marks the believer out as part of God's chosen people describes God's initiative in salvation. On the other hand, the purpose of God's work is that His people should obey Jesus Christ and this is the response He is continually looking for from believers.

i) *The achievement of Jesus Christ*
a) *His suffering and death*

Jesus Christ's blood was shed (1:2, 19). This was an event which was carefully planned by God the Father (1:20). In dying on the tree (2:24), with its reminder of the curse of God from Deuteronomy 21:22, 23, we understand Jesus to have died under God's punishment. Yet Peter is absolutely clear that He committed no sin (2:22) and was punished, therefore, for our sins (2:24; 3:18) as a once-and-for-all sacrifice, a righteous person standing in the place of unrighteous people (3:18), enabling us to know the forgiveness of all our sins. The death of Jesus Christ for sinners was therefore a penal, substitutionary death, performed voluntarily by a suffering servant (2:21ff – see Isaiah 53:1-12) as the lamb of God (1:19). The cross of our Lord Jesus Christ is therefore at the heart of the epistle.

b) His resurrection

In 1 Peter the cross is always followed by the resurrection: 1:2 / 1:3; 1:19f / 1:21; 2:24 / 2:25; 3:18 / 3:18, 21f. Christ is the living Stone (2:4) who has triumphed over death. Having been put to death in the flesh (body), He was made alive in the spirit (3:18) when God raised Him from the dead (1:21). Above all, therefore, He is the living Lord who acts as our Shepherd and Overseer (2:25) and who is looking for our obedience (1:2). Through His resurrection from the dead He is now in a position to grant new birth to His followers (1:3, 23) as they hear Him speak the good news by His Spirit (1:11) through preachers (1:12) who proclaim His Word (1:23-25).

c) His ascension

Following His resurrection, Jesus Christ went into heaven. Other New Testament writers speak of His ascension and position now seated at the right hand of the Father, but Peter dramatically highlights the significance of this journey by including other details. Not only is Jesus Christ seated in a position with all evil powers acknowledging His rule, but on the way He announced His victory to them (3:19-22). If the cross highlighted the victory of Christ over sin, and the resurrection His victory over death then His journey to heaven demonstrates His victory over evil. Together, His death, resurrection and ascension reveal the complete victory Jesus Christ has achieved.

d) His revelation / glorification

Where other New Testament writers speak of the coming or return of Jesus Christ, Peter's perspective is slightly different. Jesus Christ is present amongst His people as Shepherd (2:25) but currently unseen (1:8). Therefore, the day of His second coming is the day when His glory is revealed (1:7, 13, 21). This is the day on which believers are focused as it will usher in their salvation and inheritance (1:5, 9). It will also be the day when believers share Christ's glory (4:13; 5:4, 10). According to Peter, all the main turning points in the Christian life revolve around Jesus Christ, and salvation is not fully achieved until Jesus Christ is revealed.

(ii) Our response to Jesus Christ

a. Returning to the Shepherd

As those who have strayed from Him (2:25) through our disobedience (1:14, 18; 2:8; 3:1; 4:17) the first thing we are to do is to return to our Shepherd (2:25), and this is done by obeying His Word (1:2, 23-25). Though bound up with believing and trusting in Christ (1:8; 2:6), obedience to Christ is the more dominant note as the chief response to what God does in giving us new birth (1:3, 23). This response is evidenced by coming to Jesus Christ (2:4) and tasting His goodness (2:3).

b. Following in His footsteps

Those who have returned to their Shepherd are to follow in His steps. His life is to be an example to us (2:21), particularly in exhibiting the same response as He did amidst suffering, by refusing to retaliate (2:23; 3:9). However, it is a mindset which goes far deeper. As Jesus Christ suffered in His engagement with sin (our sin), so we are to be prepared to suffer like Him in our battle with sin (4:1). Further, as Jesus Christ demonstrated humility, so that humble attitude is to permeate the lives of all believers (3:4, 8; 5:5-7). For leaders, following the Good Shepherd will involve serving as a shepherd in the same manner as Christ Himself (5:1-4).

c. Looking forward to glory

As Christians engage fully in the world (2:11–3:7), the pattern of Christ's life – whose sufferings led to future glories – is to inform, shape and control our lives. Our sufferings due to hostility from those around us (3:13–4:6) will lead one day to sharing in Christ's glory and are therefore to be joyfully embraced (4:13; 5:1, 9, 10) in the recognition that, like Christ, we shall one day come to our destination. Our perspective is therefore always to be forward-looking as we put our confidence in what God has in store for us in the future (1:13, 21) on the day when we shall see Him (1:8, 9).

(3) *Summary*

The Lord Jesus Christ is to be the focus of our lives. Through His work and ministry our salvation is guaranteed. Through Him there is not only forgiveness of sins, but the secure prospect of future glory. He is also the pattern for how we live the Christian life today as we follow in His footsteps.

From text to teaching

(1) *Get the message clear*

Big idea (theme)

The Lord Jesus Christ is both our reigning , risen Saviour who will one day be revealed in all His glory and our example in how we live as His followers.

Big questions (aim)

Preaching or teaching on this passage should answer the following questions:

+ What did the death of Jesus Christ achieve?
+ What did the resurrection and ascension of Jesus Christ achieve?
+ How is the revelation of Jesus Christ in the future linked with our salvation?
+ How does Jesus' life serve as a guide to living the Christian life?

(2) Engage the hearer

Point of contact

If you take a ride on the London Eye it is easy to focus only on certain key buildings and neglect the rest of what is in view. Yet as you go higher you are surrounded by a wonderful panorama of London in every direction. Similarly, as we think of Jesus Christ, it is easy to focus on only one or two aspects of His work. However, what we are given in 1 Peter is a panorama, which includes every aspect of His life and achievement portrayed as an example for us.

Dominant picture

A husband might refer to his 'wife' and yet after a moment's reflection be struck by the number of roles which she plays within the life of the family: wife and lover, homemaker and carer, mother and nurse, teacher and taxi driver … and the list goes on! Similarly, we are not to be satisfied simply to refer to Jesus Christ as Lord. Through Peter's letter we have our view of Christ enriched and expanded so that we are ever more thrilled at the prospect of seeing Him when His glory is revealed.

(3) *Application*

i) In our thinking of the Christian life it is easy to think about the problems and difficulties we face due to sin, the world and the devil. We will often feel frail and weak. Yet 1 Peter encourages us to focus on what Christ has achieved and will achieve. Our salvation is completely bound up in what He has already done, and will be unveiled when He finally appears. These are the great truths in the Christian faith that never change whatever the situation. Christ has defeated sin. All powers of evil acknowledge His Lordship. He will have glory and dominion for ever and ever (4:11).

ii) Peter tells us that there is a wonderful simplicity in how we live the Christian life. We come to Jesus Christ and start obeying Him as Lord. This will be evidenced by following His example as we travel confidently to a glorious destination. Christ is not therefore only the content of our message, but also the pattern for Christian living.

Proclaiming the message
A preaching outline
Title: 'Jesus Christ In 1 Peter'
Text: **1 Peter**

Introduction 1:2
(1) *The achievement of Christ*
- *i)*   suffering and death
- *ii)* resurrection
- *iii)* ascension
- *iv)* revelation/glorification

(2) Our response to Christ
i)   returning to the Shepherd
ii) following in His footsteps
iii) looking forward to glory

Other preaching possibilities
In the exposition, attention has been given to the work of Christ and the example of Christ, but there will be others ways in which some of this important material can be presented. For example, it might be helpful to develop a series on how Peter uses the death of Christ to teach Christians how to live:

1) 1:17-21 The cross teaches us how to walk with God
2) 2:21-25 The cross teaches us how to live in difficult situations
2) 3:18-22 The cross teaches us that victory over evil is assured

Another series could consider the various titles used of Jesus Christ:

1) The living stone 2:4-8 – the stone on which to build
2) The Shepherd (and Overseer) 2:25; 5:4 – the Shepherd to follow
3) The Lord 3:15 – the Lord to revere

Leading a Bible study
Title: 'Jesus Christ In 1 Peter'
Text: 1 Peter
(1) Introduce the issues
Which aspect of the ministry of Jesus Christ do you find it easiest to neglect from His death, resurrection, ascension and final appearing?
(2) Study the passages
i)   What has Christ's death achieved for us (2:24; 3:18)?

ii) What has the resurrection of Christ achieved for us? (1:3)?

iii) Why does Peter stress the ascension of Christ in 3:19-22 and what does this add to our understanding of Christ's achievement?

iv) What are we told will happen on the day when Jesus Christ's glory is revealed (1:7-9, 13; 5:4, 10)?

v)   What is the response to Jesus Christ which Peter is looking for (1:2, 14)?

vi) In what ways is Jesus to be an example to us (2:21-23; 4:1, 2)?

vii) How does Jesus' example help us to cope with suffering? (4:12-14)?

(3) *Think it through*

i)   What would be lost if Jesus' death was only an example and not also as a substitute (2:24; 3:18)?

ii) What would be lost if we were told nothing about what happened after Jesus' resurrection (3:19-22)?

iii) What does Peter add by generally referring to conversion as obeying Christ rather than as having faith in Christ (1:2, 22-25)?

iv) Why is it so important to keep in mind the final appearing of Christ when we consider the Christian life (1:7-9, 12-14)?

(4) *Live it out*

i)   What particular aspects of Jesus Christ's ministry provide most encouragement to you at present?

ii) In what particular ways do you need to be following the example of Christ more closely?

'FURTHER RESOURCES
FOR PREACHING 1 PETER'

This book is not a commentary in the sense of fully expounding the text of 1 Peter and giving detailed justification for all the interpretations suggested. Nor is it a series of sermons on 1 Peter. Rather it gives guidance and encouragement to those who want to preach the message of 1 Peter, but are uncertain how to go about it. There are many commentaries on 1 Peter and the purpose of this brief chapter is to give some guidance on some of them and particularly to commend some which I have found useful and stimulating. It should be remembered that no single commentary will be helpful on every passage. However, commentaries can provide enormous assistance in helping us to understand the text accurately so that we can expound it effectively. Below are some suggestions with brief comments which might help in assessing whether or not a particular resource would be useful to you.

Commentaries on 1 Peter

It is worth considering having one larger commentary which can assist with most of the finer details. I have benefited considerably from the *Word Commentary* by Ramsey Michaels (Nelson, 1988). It comments on the Greek text in an extremely thorough way and in general I found it to be reliable, judicious and stimulating. If the preacher is intimidated by the Greek text then another large-scale treatment is the *New International Commentary on the New Testament* by Peter Davids (Grand Rapids, Eerdmans, 1990). Personally, I prefer the commentary by Michaels, but both are good, though there will always be places where you will want to disagree with a particular interpretation. A newer commentary which can be extremely useful is the *Baker Exegetical Commentary on the New Testament* by Karen Jobes (Grand Rapids, Baker, 2005). It is thorough, discerning and laid out in a helpful manner so that you can easily work out the structure of the letter.

Of the medium-length commentaries available, The *IVP New Testament Commentary* by Howard Marshall (Leicester, IVP, 1991) is particularly accessible and very helpful indeed. Many of the technical notes dealing with issues of interpretation appear as footnotes and I found that they were often a model of brevity and accuracy. The *Tyndale Commentary* by Wayne Grudem (Leicester, IVP, 1988) provides plenty of detail in short compass and a helpful appendix on 3:19, 20 (though ultimately I disagree with his interpretation). Though older, the previous *Tyndale Commentary* by Stibbs & Walls (Leicester, IVP, 1959) is still worth consulting especially as it includes a useful section at the end drawing together the main themes within the epistle. With its emphasis on exposition the *Bible Speaks*

Today offering by Edmund Clowney (Leicester, IVP, 1988) has plenty of helpful material and seeks to move from exegesis to exposition.

Clearly it is not possible to read everything and decisions need to be made concerning how much time you have or can make available. The preacher will want to remember that, though understanding the text is absolutely vital, yet it is only one stage in the journey to preaching a message to God's people which will encourage, strengthen, teach, train, correct and rebuke. Sometimes one commentary will help to unlock the meaning, whilst another will help your thoughts how such a message is to be applied. In this connection the commentary by *John Calvin* (Carlisle, Paternoster, 1994) can still be a helpful addition to the preacher's library.

If you have decided to embark on an expository series on 1 Peter my own suggestion would be to obtain either Michaels, Jobes or Davids, together with Marshall or Grudem.

Audio Resources
Nowadays there are opportunities to hear how others have preached 1 Peter through tape, CD or MP3 etc, such as the series preached by Phillip Jensen (Matthias Media, 1997). There is also a series preached by Simon Manchester at the Evangelical Ministry Assembly 2006 (Proclamation Trust Media). Again, such series can be educative and provide good insights concerning application. However, there is a danger that preachers will simply repeat what they have heard without first wrestling with the biblical texts themselves. Only as the Word of God dwells richly within the preacher will it start to make an impact on the life of the preacher and in turn on those who hear.

PT Media

RESOURCES FOR PREACHERS AND BIBLE TEACHERS

PT Media, a ministry of The Proclamation Trust, provides a range of multimedia resources for preachers and Bible teachers.

Books

The *Teach the Bible* commentary series, published jointly with *Christian Focus Publications*, is specifically geared to the purpose of God's Word – its proclamation as living truth. Books in this series offer practical help for preachers or teachers tackling a Bible book or doctrinal theme. Current titles are: *Teaching Matthew, Teaching John, Teaching Acts, Teaching 1 Peter, Teaching Amos* and *Teaching the Christian Hope*. Forthcoming titles include: *Teaching Mark, Teaching Daniel, Teaching Isaiah, Teaching Romans, Teaching Nehemiah, Teaching 1, 2, 3 John, Teaching Ephesians, Teaching 1&2 Samuel.*

DVDs

Preaching & Teaching the Old Testament:
        Narrative, Prophecy, Poetry, Wisdom
Preaching & Teaching the New Testament:
        Gospels, Epistles, Acts & Revelation

These interactive DVD-based training resources (including down-loadable workbooks in pdf format) are based on the core 'Principles of Exposition' element from the Cornhill Training Course. Taught by David Jackman, founder-director of Cornhill, and now President of The Proclamation Trust, the material is designed for individual study, group study or use as part of a training course.

Dick Lucas' *Instructions On Biblical Preaching* ('The Unashamed Workman') is also available on DVD.

Audio

PT Media Audio Resources offer an excellent range of material for the preacher or Bible teacher, covering over twenty years of conferences. The *Sermons On...* series (expositions) and the *Instruction On...* series (how to teach a Bible book or doctrinal theme) are available as mp3 CDs and downloads.

For further information on these and other PT Media products, visit our website at **www.proctrust.org.uk** or email **media@proctrust.org.uk**

TEACHING
AMOS

Unlocking the Prophecy of Amos
for the Bible Teacher

BOB FYALL

SERIES EDITORS: DAVID JACKMAN & ROBIN SYDSERFF

TEACHING
ACTS

Unlocking the book of Acts
for the Bible Teacher

DAVID COOK

SERIES EDITORS: DAVID JACKMAN & ROBIN SYDSERFF

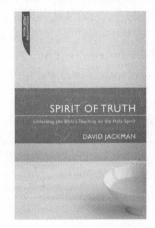

SPIRIT OF TRUTH

Unlocking the Bible's Teaching on the Holy Spirit

DAVID JACKMAN

Christian Focus Publications

publishes books for all ages
Our mission statement –

STAYING FAITHFUL

In dependence upon God we seek to help make His infallible Word, the Bible, relevant. Our aim is to ensure that the Lord Jesus Christ is presented as the only hope to obtain forgiveness of sin, live a useful life and look forward to heaven with Him.

REACHING OUT

Christ's last command requires us to reach out to our world with His gospel. We seek to help fulfil that by publishing books that point people towards Jesus and help them develop a Christ-like maturity. We aim to equip all levels of readers for life, work, ministry and mission.

Books in our adult range are published in three imprints.

Christian Focus contains popular works including biographies, commentaries, basic doctrine and Christian living. Our children's books are also published in this imprint.

Mentor focuses on books written at a level suitable for Bible College and seminary students, pastors, and other serious readers. The imprint includes commentaries, doctrinal studies, examination of current issues and church history.

Christian Heritage contains classic writings from the past.

Christian Focus Publications Ltd
Geanies House, Fearn, Ross-shire,
IV20 1TW, Scotland, United Kingdom
info@christianfocus.com
www.christianfocus.com